THE AUDACITY OF LEADERSHIP

10 ESSENTIALS TO BECOMING A TRANSFORMATIVE LEADER IN THE 21ST CENTURY

Anton J. Gunn

authorHOUSE®

AuthorHouse™
1663 Liberty Drive
Bloomington, IN 47403
www.authorhouse.com
Phone: 1-800-839-8640

Top Gunn Associates, LLC, P.O. Box 290820, Columbia, SC 29229

First published by AuthorHouse 8/24/2009

ISBN: 978-1-4490-1713-2 (e)
ISBN: 978-1-4490-1712-5 (sc)
ISBN: 978-1-4490-1711-8 (hc)

Library of Congress Control Number: 2009908299

Printed in the United States of America
Bloomington, Indiana

This book is printed on acid-free paper.

Copy Editing by Nelecia Murrell
Cover Photo by A&B Photo Service
Cover Design by Red Carpet Communications

This book is dedicated to my brother, the late Cherone L. Gunn, for demonstrating the true meaning of leadership through service and sacrifice. Without you, this book would not be possible. It's your story that has become a part of American history, which has given me the inspiration to also serve this great country. I love you and miss you, little brother.

I also dedicate this book to my wife and daughter, Tiffany and Ashley, for their love and support. I want you two to know that I love you with all of my heart.

Table of Contents

Foreword   ix
Preface   xiii
Introduction   xvii
    The Need for Audacity

Chapter One   1
    The Significance of a New Century

Chapter Two   11
    Essential Number 1: Have Vision

Chapter Three   21
    Essential Number 2: Have Commitment

Chapter Four   29
    Essential Number 3: Be Authentic

Chapter Five   41
    Essential Number 4: Learn to Listen

Chapter Six   53
    Essential Number 5: Master Selflessness

Chapter Seven   61
    Essential Number 6: Have an Emcee's Attitude

Chapter Eight   71
    Essential Number 7: Lead through Connection

Chapter Nine   79
    Essential Number 8: Build a Leadership Team

Chapter Ten   87
    Essential Number 9: Develop the Next "You"

Chapter Eleven   93
    Essential Number 10: Take Explosive Action

Chapter Twelve   99
    Conclusion

Acknowledgments   103
Appendix   105
About The Author   113
Footnotes   117

FOREWORD

As a young person, it is very hard to grasp the magnitude of words. The same applied to me as a child. But as my life progressed, I realized that words—good, bad, written, or spoken—were the fuel of deeds both good and evil. I discovered that words would have unique applications. They could become powerful road maps on the terrain of realities created by society. I learned to hold onto the words I heard during the first ten to thirteen years of my life, in the 1960s and 1970s, and to remember and grasp them like a life preserver in an ocean of confusion. In the United States, the challenge was to learn enough history to not be tricked by the cryptic, often dual, meaning of the words that we as citizens were expected to follow.

Words were especially slippery for people of color. In the black neighborhoods, "interpreters" were few, thus the myths loomed larger than the facts of the matters that affected us as a people. Hard to catch those words, much less make them mean something in our lives. Help.

I fast forward to my career as a songwriter and recording artist with the knowledge, wisdom, and understanding I got from my upbringing in my neighborhood of Roosevelt, Long Island. That sense of community supplied me with a deep respect when it comes down to the uses of words said, and words spread. Your word back then on the streets—whether "thuggin'" or "huggin'"—was considered *bond*.

Rap was the language of the streets, so to speak; lyrics were the basis of the street lingo. Thus in lyric form, I have always believed that if you know something, then you should act, rap, sing, and write like you know something. It has been the unofficial yet understood rule of "old school" entertainment. We were also aware, in the foundational period of rap music, that the culture was always to be borrowed and never owned by any one entity. Therefore, we learned that any credit taken should be immediately given those to whom it was due.

I have been given props and credit from many countries across the world for the songs I've written and the work I've committed myself to in my twenty-three years with the rap group Public Enemy. All I've said above is meant to tell you that praise is cyclical, coming full circle to give back to real people who do real things in our world.

I am a dispatcher; a messenger of information, you might say. When I would do interviews fifteen, twenty, and twenty-three years ago, I would state that Public Enemy was on a mission to raise 5,000 black leaders in the United States. I somehow underestimated that our music and those interviews were disseminated over the world wire, via the transmission of a *word*. And yet we were just reiterating the credo of the Honorable Elijah Muhammad of the Nation of Islam, that "those looking for a leader should become one." Simple enough for me. So it was imperative that Public Enemy put it out there: the *Word*, one that would be inspiring to a demographic so downtrodden and silenced in the Western world of the 1980s. We knew that especially because our words were labeled "controversial," they should be a beacon for all those with raised antennae. This meant that fans were not "fans for fans' sake": we called them "*fams*." They were, to us, the future. When I received e-mail from a fam, it was often about how he or she took this inspiration to co-sign on the already positive attributes they were raised with, to become somebody who could be a benefit to many others.

Anton Gunn has been a community organizer and an activist, and he is now a political leader serving in the South Carolina House of Representatives. Gunn is someone who, like many young black men in America, was trained to think of his future in the narrow categories prescribed to his demographic by dominant media: he would either be in entertainment or athletics. But Gunn took his athletic scholarship and parlayed it into a solid education.

He was elected in a world that changed radically in November 2008, when Barack Obama was elected president. Gunn was the political director in the pivotal state of South Carolina, a state I feel can be one of the progressive states of this new century. This is a special time with a unique situation: black men and women of color are starting to occupy key roles in government. Obama and Gunn are both true leaders, who understand the effects of their words and actions upon the masses: we know that no matter what their backgrounds, they both had to come through the tribulations and turbulence that characterizes the experience of being a young black man. And contrary to popular modern thought, I think sometimes it is okay for some leaders to talk the talk while others walk the walk: everyone is equipped with different skill sets when it comes to leadership qualities. Anton Gunn comes from the school of doing both.

Words are the revolution of now. With the portals of online convergence at our convenience, the containment of books—within this blizzard of technological and digital wizardry—will be even more significant in this new century than we first thought. This is one reason I am proud to introduce the foreword to Anton Gunn's brave, bold book about the *10 Essentials to Becoming a Transformative Leader in the 21st Century*. Leadership, power, and change are necessary for all citizens to become equal across the world in this millennium, starting with people like Anton and the commitment of his *Word*. The experiences that shaped the words in this book are undoubtedly shared by many of its future readers, and the actions they create will be shared by many of our future leaders. *The*

Audacity of Leadership is exactly the next phase for someone who recognizes who he or she truly is, and from whence they come. I'm proud to say Brother Anton Gunn has paved the next step with the necessary and inspiring *words* to take these future generations even higher, while empowering them to boldly reach down to save the rest from its lows.

Chuck D
Raptivist and cofounder of the revolutionary hip hop group Public Enemy
chuckd@publicenemy.com
www.publicenemy.com

PREFACE

I live a remarkable life. I've had opportunities to play leadership roles in places that people only dream of, and I don't take any of these experiences lightly. These experiences have molded, shaped, and helped me to frame the words written in this book.

Growing up in a military household in Virginia, I began to understand the meaning of leadership. My understanding was gained from experiences that were both right and wrong, but it was the initial inspiration of a developing culture, a blossoming art form, and an exploding music form that gave me the foundation and the framework I needed to be a transformative leader.

With age and a different living environment, these experiences were refined in South Carolina. My college football career at the state's flagship institution, the University of South Carolina (USC), played a major part in perpetuating my growth. In college, I learned from both positive and negative examples of leadership. Football coaches, as leaders of a team, are certainly supposed to exemplify leadership skills. I learned a lot from observing my coaches. After spending most of my college career on mediocre teams, I learned from them what it means to be a mediocre leader. I also learned by observing them that training for greatness is harder when you are comfortable being mediocre. However, when I was away from football coaches, but close to student leaders and my fraternity, Kappa Alpha Psi, Inc., I learned how to train for leadership at USC. While on campus, I also learned about power and the rules regarding power. I learned that power is something that we all have inside of us. It is something that we should exercise with great care and judgment. Power is the ability to lead and to define and control what happens in any given situation. I learned how to share power, and I understood how power worked within communities and organizations. These experiences prepared me to do some amazing things in my decade-long career within the state. From beginning my professional career as a community organizer, to becoming the youngest executive director of a statewide nonprofit organization, to becoming the first African American elected to the South Carolina House of Representatives for District 79, I've had some amazing opportunities.

Tragedy has also been a vital experience that taught me a great deal about leadership. In October of 2000, my younger brother, Seaman Cherone Louis Gunn, was killed in an Al-Qaeda terrorist attack aboard the USS *Cole* at the Port of Aden in Yemen. This attack, which took the life of my brother and sixteen of his shipmates, was devastating to my family and our community. Personally, this tragedy pulled back the scab of failed leadership in the highest ranks of our military structure and in our federal government. This attack showed the failures of those who were responsible for protecting our personnel overseas. It also showed the failure of those "leaders" who were also responsible for investigating terrorist attacks. However, from this tragedy, I was afforded the opportunity to speak to leaders who were in very powerful positions in our country, including the commander of the U.S. Atlantic Fleet, Robert Natter; director of the Federal Bureau of Investigation, Louis Freeh; the attorneys general of the United States of America, Janet Reno and John Ashcroft; chairman of the Joint Chiefs of Staff, Hugh Shelton; dozens of senior officers in the United States military; and even the President of the United States, Bill Clinton. In meeting with these leaders, I gained a very diverse perspective about how to conduct leadership in crisis, but most importantly, when and how leaders fail in their duties. This tragedy had a strong impact on my definition of leadership and how I define transformative leadership in this book.

The most profound experience that I have had in my life as a leader is the opportunity to work directly with, to learn from, and to play a role in the political career of the first African American president in history of these United States. I was one of the first people to serve on the campaign staff of Barack Obama. I was the first person hired to help manage his campaign in the state of South Carolina. Serving as the political director, I was directly involved in the planning, decision-making, and the grassroots leadership development of this now legendary campaign. Working sometimes eighteen hours a day, with a team of people who were on an unrelenting mission to support and elevate a leader who we believed would change politics forever, was life changing. My year-long journey with Barack Obama was one of the most wonderful and profound experiences of my life. To watch a man go from a new, fresh face in the United States Senate, to become a long-shot presidential candidate, to become the victor in races that many people thought were impossible, was astounding. What is extremely astounding to me is how I got the role as one of the linchpins in the election campaign, which changed the pages of history. What's even more significant is the fact that I was given the opportunity to be there, to witness the stumbles along the way, to watch the changes, and to see the leadership growth—this experience was truly unforgettable. These profound encounters are important to me because they have helped hone my personal leadership development process. They were even more significant because by watching, learning from, and modeling Barack Obama, who is undoubtedly an example of a transformative leader in the twenty-first century, I have developed a foundation to do more than I could ever imagine.

This book is intended to provide some simple concepts, through a contemporary format, and these pages underscore what I have learned from my life. Each chapter begins with a quote or phrase that I have used to channel my knowledge and understanding of the concepts herein. Essentially, the quotes I have chosen, which come from various historical and present-day leaders, emphasize the fundamental attributes of a transformative leader. In addition to exploring the key components of leadership, I have also included an example of someone who has directly and indirectly taught me a great deal—someone I have been able to model my life after. This person's examples have laid the foundation for the concepts that frame *The Audacity of Leadership*. And I believe it is the audacity of the transformative leader in the twenty-first century that will ultimately define leadership for our generation.

By nature, I am an optimist, and I am excited about what the future holds for our country. I am also excited about what the future can hold for those who read these pages, understand the concepts herein, and apply them to their lives. These are the concepts that have helped frame, shape, and prepare me to continue seeking the higher levels of leadership in our country. These concepts can prepare you for leadership in life and within your organization. Together we can positively transform our world.

> "Everyone thinks of changing the world, but no one thinks of changing himself."

-Leo Tolstoy

INTRODUCTION

THE NEED FOR AUDACITY

In the world of ants, worker ants have one purpose: to work. They find food and build a grand colony for the queen. Ants know their role in society. They do their job because it is the job they were born to do. Their role never changes. Worker ants are not innovators or thinkers, nor do they strive to be. They don't create a new job or seek a higher purpose. They work. They dig. They get food. They serve the queen. And when they have served their purpose, they die.

In the ant world, everyone focuses on the queen. She finds a suitable nesting site and will urgently dig herself a tunnel, ending in a small chamber. She will seal herself in and, unless forced to, never emerge into the sunlight again. Workers live only to serve, provide for, and protect her. The queen makes the decisions on where the workers live and where they move, and then she decides when to replace the workers by laying eggs for new workers. Without thought, the queen determines the life and death of the worker ant.

In our current world, most leaders function like queen ants. They make the decisions and expect the workers under them to follow, because that is what they were born to do: *follow*. These leaders work from their own framework. In essence, today's leaders seal themselves in a small chamber with limited access to worker ants. They are isolated from those they represent and seek the counsel of only a few to make a decision. The relationship between leaders and their followers has functioned in this manner for decades.

The average citizen is often disconnected from those in our society who are in leadership positions. In absence of such a connection, people will follow orders and the direction of these leaders, having been blindly cut off from the organizational hierarchy, which are the platforms on which leaders stand. As a result, people become the worker ants. They function as workers, plodding through every day, keeping themselves occupied like worker ants. There is very little time to seek out a higher purpose. Essentially, the sole purpose of the average citizen is to work, and like worker ants, their deeds and death will go unsung, leaving room for the next worker to happily take his place.

When I played college football, sweating in the hot South Carolina summers, I learned that our football program could only succeed as a team, but to succeed as a team we also had to prepare ourselves individually—mentally and physically. It also required us to follow the direction of our leader, the coach. Well, after two years of doing everything our coaches asked to prepare ourselves and work hard as teammates to succeed, we continued to come up short. We lost a lot more games than we won. It was frustrating to be a worker, giving all we had, but feeling as if we never had good direction toward victory—never having good leadership that could teach us how to win. Through those experiences, I came to one conclusion—I refuse to lose anymore. **I refuse to just be a worker ant!**

Have you ever thought or asked yourself: **What type of ant will I be?** Will you find pleasure and comfort in busying yourself with the predictable task of a worker or will you position yourself to assume a new role—one who breaks the rules of this caste leadership society?

Through my life's experience, I have learned to make decisions for myself and thereby will leave a mark on the world when I am gone. My mark will be to leave behind a better world than I was born into. Leaders should want to give people hope, aspirations, dreams, and goals. I refer to this as a new transformative change in the lives of people. This is the challenge leaders should put forth. I challenge you to live your life like this. I challenge you to live focused on change. I challenge you to focus on starting something new. Be bold toward a new beginning, no differently than the American forefathers who, I believe, were tired of being worker ants for King George III. They wanted change. They wanted freedom to think, serve, and act in a greater power. They wanted to help themselves so they could help others. They wanted new and better lives, different and more purposeful than the ones they were living. It was in this spirit that our forefathers had the audacity to start a revolution. They were driven to that revolution, and that revolution has driven us to become the greatest nation in the world. It is this audacious spirit of revolution that drives me. It is also through this spirit that I want to change the world. Through my actions, words, and service, I have the audacity of leadership. By applying the principles explained in the following chapters, I am certain you will emerge as a world changer. This book provides the blueprint you need to make this change possible.

As Leo Tolstoy said, change must start with thinking about you. *The Audacity of Leadership* is a frame of essential qualities that upon mastering, *you* can become a transformative leader to impact change. To live a life that is transformative, you have to be willing to perform the ground work. You must:

- ✓ Have a vision that is inclusive and compelling
- ✓ Demonstrate your commitment to become an audacious leader
- ✓ Illuminate your authenticity to the point of unquestionable truth

✓ Listen in special ways to address all concerns, spoken and unspoken

✓ See yourself as a bold leader, with boldness to go where no leader has gone before

✓ Be willing to seriously and consistently serve and help others, which in turn encourages others to follow your lead

✓ Develop a dream team leadership community that will challenge, support, and replenish your leadership skills

✓ Build strong relationships with the individuals in your organization so that people will not quit on you

✓ Develop the next generation of audacious leaders as you develop yourself

✓ Take action and have the faith and confidence to make change

I affirm that these skills create transformative leaders. We need leaders who will right wrongs rather than compound them. We need leaders who will surround themselves with a team of people who can complement them where they may be weak, and challenge them in areas of strength to make them stronger. I want leaders who are selfless in their pursuit to help others. I strive to be that kind of leader. I want you to be that kind of leader, too. Everyone has the ability to become a transformative leader in some way.

You may be thinking that these are naïve desires or a utopian view of leadership development. But, at your core, do you wonder if it could work? Our culture has grown accustomed to the belief that very few leaders can live up to these standards, which is the very proof that poor leadership has corrupted our sense of government, business, and community. Selfish leadership created this memory loss regarding the basic function of a democratic society. Our democratic society should be *by the people and for the good of the people*, yet many who exist in a democratic society have grown to expect the contrary—we have been led to believe it's intended for the people in theory, but in reality our democratic government fuels the prosperity of the "few."

In turn, society as a whole feeds this sense of selfishness. We have created a "me" society. We seemingly march to the mantra of survival of the fittest, and every man for himself. We are told if we want to make a mark or make something of ourselves, we have to focus only on ourselves. The idea of teamwork has been reduced to a one-man show. The attitude of the day is to "look out for number one and be sure to step on the person who is number two." Even the process of *rising* to leadership appears to have become corrupt. Some people, greedy for power, are willing to do anything to secure their way to the top. Consequently, it seems the only way to succeed is to adopt that corruptive behavior. Potential leaders are encouraged to be disconnected and, at times, corrupt. Leaders have been willing to compromise integrity for some personal gain. The philosophy of building transformative leaders through building strong communities appears dead. This current process of leadership is contrary to the very fabric that led our forefathers to create our great nation.

True leadership warrants service. Twenty-first-century leadership requires commitment, inspiration, and authenticity. Leaders should also be visionaries with values, who endure the challenges to ultimately share the benefits. Having vision, sharing values, and meeting challenges creates new ideas to solve problems. Leaders should also be inclusive; building bridges that help the world go in a positive direction. Understanding The Audacity of Leadership can bring you into this power source.

Audacity is a new leadership framework that engages leaders and empowers "ordinary" citizens to take ownership for innovative and transformative change. Audacity provides leaders a new perspective to maintain the integrity of their leadership while empowering others. Finally, it gives every individual the power to contribute his or her talents to our society, and in doing so, we can achieve extraordinary things for the world community.

Your skills, talents, and abilities are gifts that you should give to others. This book is designed to give you the tools to harness those gifts into a movement of people power. Inspiration creates motivation; motivation breaks stagnation and builds innovation. Audacity is the inspiration you need to motivate you to live out your fullest leadership potential.

I am not the first to dream this dream of leadership. There were many before me who strived to be this brand of leader. The late Senator Paul Wellstone succeeded.

> A few weeks ago, I got off the plane, and as we were driving to Tunica, Mississippi, they said to me, "First we're going to go to the elementary school and you will address the third and fourth graders on the last day of class." I said, "Address? On the last day of school?" But I said okay, and we went there. I asked the children, do you like school? What's important about it? And one young girl said, "It's important because I can be what I want to be." And I said, "What do you want to be?" And then there were forty hands up, and the rest of the hour was students talking about what they want to be. One of them wanted to be a psychiatrist. Or a doctor. Or a professional wrestler. Or a professional basketball player. Or a teacher. Or an artist. Or a business person, on and on and on. Those children had hope.[1]

> **Senator Paul D. Wellstone'**
> **Iowa State, July 11, 1998**

We must create a world where these children's hopes can amount to more than an unattainable dream. If we apply the principles within these pages, we can see how to bring their dreams to fruition. We will see how leadership can bring the hope and the possibility of a better world. The model of leadership we hope to see is right in front of us; we just have to understand how to look for it.

Most are familiar with the logo of FedEx. The bright colored letters mark boxes, trucks, and airplanes all around the world. But can you see beyond the letters themselves? Within these letters is an arrow—a symbol of new direction and change; a symbol of forward movement to the next level, place, or destination. If you examine the logo through a different lens, the new direction can be seen between the "E" and the "X"—an arrow. That unnoticed arrow has always been between those letters. My point is, just because you have never seen yourself as a transformational, audacious leader doesn't mean that it can't be found in you. There is audacious leadership in every one of us. This model of leadership is already happening everywhere ... you just have to know how to look for it.

> "Change will not come if we wait for some other person or some other time. We are the ones we've been waiting for. We are the change that we seek."
>
> -President Barack Obama

CHAPTER ONE

THE SIGNIFICANCE OF A NEW CENTURY

A s we approach the conclusion of the first decade of the twenty-first century, we must recognize that we are in an era of great change. The world in which we live is constantly evolving at a rapid pace, whether we are referring to changes in technology, our environment, our culture, or our economic foundation. This is evident just in the first ten years of the twenty-first century, in which events occurred that we have not encountered in the history of our planet. Whether it is touch-screen cell phones, interdependency of the world financial markets, or airline security, our world has dramatically changed.

The changes that have occurred in this era are testaments of the great progress we have made. But as we closely examine the first decade of this new century, it is clear that some of our leaders have not shared in the positive change. Numerous examples of poor leadership, ranging from the War on Terror and the global oil crisis to the corporate financial crisis, have become the rule instead of the exception. These failures in leadership occurred right before our eyes, and our country was not prepared for the devastation that followed. Naturally, in our desperation, we sought the help of other leaders, but they also consistently let us down. Instead of gaining assistance, we found our religious leaders engaging in inappropriate relationships, teachers having sexual relationships with their students, corporate CEOs abusing their power, investment bankers stealing from pension funds, and political leaders becoming morally bankrupt and corrupt.

Consequently, their inconsistency forced us into a place of complete frustration and utter exhaustion. We are in need of change, but we approach this change with great hesitation, for fear that the grass may not be greener on the other side. Our uncertainty tends to give way to fear because we do not know who or what to trust.

So we continue to ask, "When will these troubled times end? Who will lead us out of the despairing state we're in?" Before now, most would answer these questions with a simple phrase, "I don't know." Today, I would like to challenge you to consider yourself as the answer; consider how you can contribute to creating the positive change we need; consider how you can become an instrumental part of the new era of twenty-first-century leaders.

What citizens of our country need more than anything else is someone who will be there, especially during times of crisis. People need confidence in their leaders. They need to have the understanding that there is someone who can bring strength, stability, and guidance during turbulent times. People are seeking out leaders with principles who will stand up in this era and give them the assurance that no matter what may go wrong, or how afraid they may become in the midnight hour, everything will be all right. They are looking for spiritual, emotional, political, intellectual, and economical direction. People are desperate for the confidence of a leader who is rational, equipped, and well-prepared to lead them through these uncertain times.

They have no confidence in many of our current leaders because many of them limit themselves to archaic concepts and neglect the demands of our present age. They see no need to push the envelope. They shun progressive thinking, and they find it unnecessary to challenge the status quo by boldly going where other leaders have been afraid to go. So it is time for a new legion of leaders to rise up and assume the position of transformation.

To become a transformative leader you must first recognize and understand the changes currently taking place. However, you must also recognize and understand the problems of the past—the mistakes that other leaders made—so that you can entertain ways to correct their wrongs. In addition to understanding the past and present, you must take the time to understand what people seek in leadership so that you can ultimately discover and meet their needs. But in order to develop these skills, you must possess a discipline that fuels your work ethic to relentlessly pursue your vision.

The historical context of a new century leader can be traced back to twentieth-century America. The twentieth century was an amazing time of growth and change. The face of the global community was changing—a change that began in our country. America was at the heart of that change as it relates to invention, experimentation, industrial innovation, and political leadership. There were people at the forefront of the revolution that transformed America into a diverse melting pot. The twentieth century was the beginning of a new era—one that forced the world to recognize the United States of America as an independent world power. We won the battle over the Western frontier and settled the country from coast to coast. We built a railroad that stretched across the continent, connecting one coast to the other. We drilled for oil and eventually became a world power in the petroleum markets. We produced steel in record numbers and in record time. In addition to our overall development, we were pioneers of the gasoline engine and the automobile. The telephone was created to make communication more accessible, and skyscrapers went from being scribbled on blueprints to forming new skylines of our cities. Americans like Andrew Carnegie, John D. Rockefeller, Susan B. Anthony, J. P. Morgan, Jane Addams, Theodore Roosevelt, Booker T. Washington, Joseph Pulitzer, Alexander Graham Bell, and Henry Ford are among the few extraordinary individuals who used their innovative ideas to transform American culture. These individuals were willing to be the change they wanted to see, and in doing so, they managed to lay the foundation for the next century.

These leaders changed America forever. They each had an individual style and framework as a leader. But what they possessed, which left an indelible mark on America, was a vision dedicated to bettering the lives of the American people. Their authenticity, coupled with their ability to empower others, made them transformative leaders—these men and women were among the group of audacious leaders who transformed twentieth-century America.

It is my belief that in the twenty-first century, we have the same opportunity to bring about transformation. We must take full advantage of the charge before us to improve the lives and lifestyles of the American people. To accomplish this transformative task, we must be led by a group of transformative leaders. These leaders must be transformative in every field of human endeavors (e.g., business, politics, and religious communities). They must have a level of audacity that's unmatched, similar to the audacity of the great leaders at the turn of twentieth century.

So ask yourself, am I the transformative leader twenty-first-century America has been waiting for? Can I lend a positive contribution to our nation's progression? We all have the opportunity to assume the position of a transformative leader, but we have to decide whether we will actively participate or passively dissipate. I made the decision as a youngster to become an active participant through the guidance of one of my role models from hip hop music, Public Enemy. One of Public Enemy's messages was, "If you don't know your past, you don't know where you are going in the present."[2] I assert if you don't know your present, you cannot predict your future. We must look back to understand our greatness, in that it only took us one hundred years to revolutionize the world. We've done so much and come so far. When we examine our present, it is evident that we are facing uncertain times. However, the beauty of it all is that we have the power to decide where we go from here.

I firmly believe that the turn of the century provides us the opportunity to make a significant change—at the beginning of a new century, people expect something different. They expect a bold, new perspective; they expect a challenge; they expect change. Therefore, just as a group of audacious, transformative leaders propelled America to challenge and change the world at the beginning of the twentieth century, our moral and civic responsibility is to challenge and change the world of the twenty-first century. But we can only accomplish this task through authentic, transformative leadership.

One doesn't have to look far to see what transformative leadership did for our nation at the turn of the century. Just turn on your computer and search the White House Web site. The biography of the twenty-sixth president, Theodore Roosevelt, provides a picture-perfect example of audacious transformative leadership.

PRESIDENT THEODORE ROOSEVELT AT THE TURN OF THE TWENTIETH CENTURY.[3]

With the assassination of President McKinley, Theodore Roosevelt, not quite 43, became the youngest president in the Nation's history. He brought new excitement and power to the Presidency, as he vigorously led Congress and the American public toward progressive reforms and a strong foreign policy.

He took the view that the president as a "steward of the people" should take whatever action necessary for the public good unless expressly forbidden by law or the Constitution. "I did not usurp power," he wrote, "but I did greatly broaden the use of executive power."

Roosevelt's youth differed sharply from that of the Log Cabin presidents. He was born in New York City in 1858 into a wealthy family, but he too struggled--against ill health--and in his triumph became an advocate of the strenuous life.

In 1884 his first wife, Alice Lee Roosevelt, and his mother died on the same day. Roosevelt spent much of the next two years on his ranch in the Badlands of Dakota Territory. There he mastered his sorrow as he lived in the saddle, driving cattle, hunting big game--he even captured an outlaw. On a visit to London, he married Edith Carow in December 1886.

During the Spanish-American War, Roosevelt was lieutenant colonel of the Rough Rider Regiment, which he led on a charge at the Battle of San Juan. He was one of the most conspicuous heroes of the war.

Boss Tom Platt, needing a hero to draw attention away from scandals in New York State, accepted Roosevelt as the Republican candidate for governor in 1898. Roosevelt won and served with distinction.

As president, Roosevelt held the ideal that the Government should be the great arbiter of the conflicting economic forces in the Nation, especially between capital and labor, guaranteeing justice to each and dispensing favors to none.

Roosevelt emerged spectacularly as a "trust buster" by forcing the dissolution of a great railroad combination in the Northwest. Other antitrust suits under the Sherman Act followed.

Roosevelt steered the United States more actively into world politics. He liked to quote a favorite proverb, "Speak softly and carry a big stick."

Aware of the strategic need for a shortcut between the Atlantic and Pacific, Roosevelt ensured the construction of the Panama Canal. His corollary to the Monroe Doctrine prevented the establishment of foreign bases in the Caribbean and arrogated the sole right of intervention in Latin America to the United States.

He won the Nobel Peace Prize for mediating the Russo-Japanese War, reached a Gentleman's Agreement on immigration with Japan, and sent the Great White Fleet on a goodwill tour of the world.

Some of Theodore Roosevelt's most effective achievements were in conservation. He added enormously to the national forests in the West, reserved lands for public use, and fostered great irrigation projects.

He crusaded endlessly on matters big and small, exciting audiences with his high-pitched voice, jutting jaw, and pounding fist. "The life of strenuous endeavor" was a must for those around him, as he romped with his five younger children and led ambassadors on hikes through Rock Creek Park in Washington, D.C.

Leaving the Presidency in 1909, Roosevelt went on an African safari, then jumped back into politics. In 1912 he ran for president on a Progressive ticket. To reporters he once remarked that he felt as fit as a bull moose, the name of his new party.

So the question remains, can you follow Roosevelt's example of transformative leadership? Are you prepared to transform the twenty-first century as he transformed the twentieth century? Are you progressive in your vision and ideals to frame what we can accomplish together? Are you willing to surround yourself with people who can help you become a transformative leader? I wrote this book with the hope you might gain some inspiration from my experiences to propel you to pursue transformative leadership. These pages contain a synopsis of my journey to becoming a transformative leader, and I believe it will spur you to begin (or continue) your journey toward transformative leadership.

We've been given an opportunity to positively change our world, and because this change is demanding, few will assume the responsibilities of a twenty-first-century leader. However, as you journey through the pages of this book, consider this: Will you be one of the few? Will you take the opportunity to bring about change? Will you be a twenty-first-century leader who transforms our country, our world, and our planet for the next one hundred years?

Throughout the last decade, I spent a significant amount of time as a community organizer in South Carolina, working on issues that affect people. I took a community-based approach to addressing and solving issues such as health care, education, economic development, job training, and poverty. I spent a good bit of my time going door-to-door in communities, talking to residents about their hopes, dreams, challenges, and concerns. My ultimate goal was to help people understand what's happening in their communities, to find out the common community problems, and to work with them to create solutions.

People were excited about addressing issues that mattered to them, bringing a beam of hope that positive change in their respective communities was possible. Usually the arbiter who could solve their problems was a local elected official. Much to my dismay, the hard work was not always associated with finding a solution to a problem. The work was getting people to believe that their local leader was caring, committed, and honest enough to let them know that he or she was going to assist in finding a solution to meet the needs of their community. I would take them to see their local politicians. I would help community residents try to convince their local politician to do something about the problems in their neighborhoods. Each time, we came away disappointed. Instead of politicians trying to solve the problems brought by the community residents, they would resort to giving lip service to their concerns. These leaders would tell the citizens anything to ease their concerns, but their failure to act in solving these issues left in place a destructive status quo.

At the time, I couldn't understand why these leaders would get excited about maintaining the status quo. They were keeping communities oppressed by not making progress and changes that actually mattered to the people they represented. Despite their ineffectiveness, these leaders maintained their position of power.

These instances caused me to realize that many of these citizens had leaders who did not understand their struggles, challenges, or life experiences. This was a classic example of disconnect between the queen ant and the worker ants. As a result, I decided to become their advocate. I decided to use my resources and skills to convince those leaders to take action. Even with compelling arguments, I came away from these encounters having failed to achieve progress.

Frustrated with the ineffectiveness of local politicians for nearly a decade in South Carolina, I decided to change my course of action. I thought to myself, instead of asking politicians to do the right thing, and watching them refuse every promising proposal every year, instead of asking them to have compassion and understanding about what's happening to people in South Carolina, I could do the job better. The diversity of my experiences in the communities of this state was needed to bring about positive transformation—I made a decision to run for public office.

In 2006, I decided to run for the South Carolina House of Representatives. Political pundits told me that I was wasting my time. Political pundits told me that it would not be possible for a thirty-three-year-old African American professional, who was a Democrat, to run and win in a district that had been held by Republicans for twenty-two years. The incumbent was popular and seasoned. Political pundits told me it would not be possible for an African American to actually win an election in a district that had never elected an African American; that something of this manner had never happened in the history of South Carolina politics. I found comfort in entertaining the fact that we were in a new era of American politics. I believed this era of American politics would bring about change because it was comprised of people who believed, as I did, that a leader who possesses a clear vision to bring people together for the sake of creating a better future was a worthy cause. In essence, I saw myself as a transformative leader, and I was running as a new leader fit for the twenty-first century. After all, I believe that change is a byproduct of what we can do together! My overall message to the voters was, "The leadership you want is the change that you deserve."

My campaign was considered, by many, to be a nontraditional campaign for an African American candidate in South Carolina. I ran in a majority-white district (68 percent white/32 percent African American). It consisted of middle class and upper middle class residents. Household incomes ranged $50,000 to $90,000 per year. The district's average income was at least twice as high as the average South Carolinian. The district was suburban and rural. There's no inner city, no high-rise buildings, and no public housing. It was growing and changing; new families were moving in from the Northeast, the Midwest, and the West Coast, and African American families were moving into the middle class bracket. There was a changing dynamic in the district, one that gave me a good chance of winning if I ran against the twelve-year incumbent.

On November 8, 2006, after the votes were tallied, I lost by 298 votes. Political pundits were enamored that I came so close to making history. And two years later, after that narrow loss, I became the history-making state legislator who represents this wonderful House district. I made history because I realized that the era was changing and it was time to seize the opportunity. During this time, I became what I had always been: the transformative leader that I looked for in others.

...Where There is No Vision, The People Perish

-Proverbs 29:18

CHAPTER TWO

ESSENTIAL NUMBER 1: HAVE VISION

Transformative leadership is built on *vision*. You must first be able to see where the end zone is located on the football field before you attempt to score a touchdown. Taking action to do something without a sense of what you hope to accomplish in the end will undoubtedly jeopardize the future of the individual group, organization, or business you hope to lead. So it is very important that you design a clear roadmap to avoid potential disaster along the way. Your vision is the roadmap to guide you to success. By having vision as a guide, you will increase your chances of becoming a transformative leader.

Vision is the diversity of one's life experience that gives the ability to understand the past and present of a situation, and organize a mental picture of its future. Within this picture, one must be able to see how that new vision is better than the past or the present visions. Twenty-first-century leaders must be able to understand the situations of the past, and the problems of the present, in order to chart out a course that will lead people toward a better future.

Knowing the past, present, and possible future is critical for the success of a twenty-first-century leader. No longer is it feasible to only look at the *current* status of a business, organization, church, or community to effectively chart a new course toward its future. This will cause you to make short-sighted decisions that could lead to extreme, unintended consequences. Therefore, it is important that the leader has an understanding of the past. Having a clear understanding of the past and present will enable a leader to paint the overall picture of a future.

Also, in order to have vision about where you would like to lead an individual group, organization, or business, you must have first-hand experience. For instance, if you have aspirations to become the transformative chief executive officer of a major corporation, you must spend time and gain experience working in that corporation (or one like it). You must be exposed to the company's mode of operation and values, as well as experience all that it has to offer before you can become the head. It is only at this point that you may potentially possess the wisdom to advance the company's endeavors as CEO. Likewise, in order to be an effective minister or pastor of a church organization and share your vision where you would like to lead the congregation, you must first be evangelized, baptized, and ordained in that particular faith community. Therefore, it is not possible to impart vision without ample training and experience, because the vision is shaped by your personal experience.

In the twenty-first century, you must have relevant experiences to birth a promising vision. You must first know what is ineffective before proposing a potentially effective plan toward a solution. Transformative leaders gain their inspiration for a new vision from the trials and tribulations of their life's experiences. As Frederick Douglass appropriately stated, without struggle there is no progress. I assert that this holds true for leaders. If leaders have never experienced struggle in life, then they will not make progress in their leadership abilities. So a transformative leader must have experienced struggle and learned from those troubling experiences to propose changes that will promote progress.

If you desire to lead with an inspirational, decisive, contextual vision as your guide, you must build on the knowledge that you have ascertained from life experiences. You're able to cultivate and impart profitable viewpoints when you have been exposed to a plethora of different experiences. So when you are exposed to tasks that have failed, you will be able to use the pieces of your varied experiences to set a vision in motion that could ultimately reverse the wrongs (within your business, company, church—your world). Therefore, to birth a vision that has a positive impact on your world, you must be clothed with experience.

LEADERS NEED VISION

Vision is a powerful force for anyone seeking leadership in life. But to be a transformative leader, vision is essential. A vision is a goal toward which a leader focuses energy and resources. Remaining focused on the vision keeps a leader moving forward despite obstacles, setbacks, fear of failure, and hardships (such as negative responses from colleagues, the media, or the uninformed public— even if you are faced with a bankruptcy, job loss, divorce, or political defeats, you must stay focused on the vision). The lesson for a leader with vision is, when things go wrong, do not go wrong with them. You have to remain steady.

Once a leader has conceived the vision, he or she must be able to share it. A leader must be able to articulate the vision so that everyone can understand it. People must know where the leader wants to take the group, so the leader must be able to communicate that vision. In order to effectively communicate, you must master language. You do not need to be well versed in the queen's English, but you need to be able to articulate your vision in words, pictures, and objects to which other people can connect. People will connect to your vision, but they must also see themselves as a part of it. Transformative leaders want individuals to take ownership of the vision.

Finding people who will willingly believe in your vision is only made possible through a leader's communication. Leaders can possess great vision, but if they fail to communicate their vision, it instantly becomes obsolete. For example, if an artist paints a picture, but never reveals it, no one will be inspired by it. No one will find it engaging, and no one will be captured by the possibilities it invokes. Consequently, a vision is essentially nullified if it is not mobilized through some form of communication.

In addition to painting and articulating the big picture, a leader must get each individual to see themselves within the vision. After painting the big picture, most would acknowledge the need for a vision for change. Most would acknowledge the place in the future where your organization, church, or community needs to go. However, many may not be able to envision themselves as being a vital part of the team that makes that vision a reality, . It then becomes the task of the leader to enable each individual to see how he or she is a key component of the whole. To every whole, there are parts, and without the parts, there will be no whole. The leader must communicate that each individual is needed—each person places an important part in materializing the vision.

A transformative leader's vision must be infectious. Vision is the cornerstone that one builds a foundation of a team on. Vision adds meaning to the team. It adds purpose. When people understand a leader's vision, they understand what the organization is trying to accomplish and what it stands for. Everyone can see what the future holds for him or her within that organization. The vision must be simple, rational, and attainable. The vision must be far-reaching and creative—it should stretch and capture the imaginations of all individuals involved in the materialization process. And when opposition arises, the team will press forward, believing that the end results are possible.

However, you should plan with the end in mind—that is the vision. Great leaders of the twenty-first century must know how to paint the picture. They need to paint a big picture that inspires, engages, and captures the excitement of what is possible.

President Barack Obama is certainly a man who understands transformative leadership, especially as it relates to *vision*. By culminating his life experiences, he has seemingly set a vision in motion that has impacted the world. He was raised in Hawaii, which has a diverse community that is unlike mainstream America. He initially attended Occidental College on the West Coast, then he moved to the East Coast to attended Columbia University. His journey from Hawaii, to Los Angeles, through New York landed him ultimately on the South Side of Chicago. Barack Obama worked diligently to improve the lives of poor families on the South Side. Following Obama's time in Chicago, he moved to Cambridge, Massachusetts, to attend Harvard Law School. Thereafter, he returned to Chicago with a burning desire to continue his work of helping people improve their communities. It is from this point we know the historic story that has become President Barack Obama. Each experience that Obama encountered ultimately served as a piece of the map he used to guide him—these experiences are the main ingredients that shaped his *vision* for a better America. Since he was exposed to various cultural and socioeconomic groups, he could formulate a *vision* that was inclusive of all Americans and a *vision* that would address the needs of the American people.

Then-Senator Barack Obama painted a clear vision for where he thought America should go in his book entitled *The Audacity of Hope.*[4] He brought the picture of the American Dream to life through its pages. He painted the big picture of the unifying problems in America and where he thought America needs to go to solve these problems in the twenty-first century. The book was also a picture that he used to paint small stories and small issues so that people could see themselves in the vision. His book addressed a number of issues (e.g., politics, faith, race, the military, and where America exists in the world). The single thread connecting these issues was the idea that we all have values. Our values are the veins that bring life to our democracy. He laid out simple stories that just about every person could see themselves in the big picture of an improved America—and this picture ultimately led America to trust him with leading our country.

He also painted a big picture vision in his campaign; this vision encompassed a lot of details and a lot of issues, but what made him successful is that he was able to crystallize the vision into small issues like the war, health care, the economy, and even race so people could see themselves within that vision. These small issues were discussed in small settings on the campaign trail and in peoples' homes. Obama's campaign strategy focused on allowing individuals to talk very personally about what was wrong in America. They were also able to express what was happening in their lives, which came about as a result of America's wrongs. Whether it was having a child in Iraq, living without access to health insurance, suffering from unemployment, being unable to pay for college, or feeling anger concerning how public education looked in various communities, people expressed their personal pain about the current state of America.

From this point forward, the public, who had personalized their problems in America, were eager to create a solution. Barack Obama then painted a picture of what he thought could be done about all of those problems if he was President of the United States. His campaign message was that of a new America, which valued giving people the power to address their problems. It was this message and vision that inspired a generation and changed the history of American politics.

During the 2004 presidential primary, Americans expressed great frustration with the issues the nation faced and the way in which government officials chose to address them. They showed discontent with the War on Terror, the Patriot Act, and immigration issues. However, the thing that was disconcerting to me was that no one addressed the issue of poverty in America. No one seemed concerned with the lack of education and health care, the reasons why people were poor, and the need to end poverty in America.

At the time, I was the director of a small nonprofit organization in South Carolina, working on consumer issues. I considered the issue at hand, poverty. I thought the only way to be heard was to capture the ear of the presidential candidates. We needed them to talk about poverty issues; 34 million people in America were victims of poverty, and these staggering statistics could not go unnoticed. The last time a presidential candidate or president had uttered a word about poverty, in a positive sense, was in 1964 when President Lyndon Johnson passed the War on Poverty Program.

Thereafter, Ronald Reagan addressed people who fraudulently posed themselves as poor to abuse government aid (e.g., welfare services). But there had been no positive conversations about what we should do to eradicate poverty since President Johnson.

As a result, I thought we needed to create a forum, not a debate, but a venue where the presidential candidates could openly address the issue of poverty right here in South Carolina—this was my *vision*. I gathered a group of my peers, men and women who worked daily on issues of poverty, and said to them, "What do you think about putting a forum together to get the presidential candidates in a room here in South Carolina to address issues of poverty in twenty-minute intervals?" Their immediate feedback was, "You must be crazy! No presidential candidate would show. You might get Dennis Kucinich, but you'll never get John Kerry, John Edwards, or Howard Dean. They will not be interested in coming to address these issues. They are too busy running for president. We represent poor people, and poor people don't vote. They would not be interested in coming our way." They were unable to see my vision because the circumstances at hand blurred their lenses.

It then became my responsibility to paint a clear picture that would convince them to believe that this forum was possible. I challenged them to think about the issue of poverty—poverty did not just impact "poor people." For example, there were schoolteachers who could not perform their jobs effectively because their students came from communities that were not receiving the support and services they needed to perform proficiently in the classroom. We needed to get the next leader of the free world to come to an event where we discussed poverty and ways we could solve this issue. We needed to present the varied dimensions of poverty: health care, education, immigration, job training, and housing. I painted the following picture: "It would be great if we had an American president who not only understood poverty issues but actually adopted an agenda to solve these issues. What would the world be like if we ended poverty in America; if no one was hungry, homeless, or uneducated?" They then responded, "That would be great but ..."—before they could entertain the "BUT," I interrupted their thought process, saying, "The only way we're going to get to that place is to get the candidates in a room and talk to them about poverty." They then questioned, "How can we do that?" As it became evident that they had begun to buy into the vision, I elaborated by saying, "We need to rally a team of people to host an event to bring all the presidential candidates together." Then I successfully recruited my peers to join me in my efforts to get the presidential candidates to address poverty in America.

We proceeded to knock on the doors of various groups such as the AFL-CIO, the NAACP, the National Education Association, and other nonprofit groups. When approaching these groups, I asked them to consider what America would be like if the issues that ailed them were addressed, issues such as lack of job opportunities, equal rights, poor access to health care, and quality schools. They instantly expressed interest in joining our efforts because they saw how they could directly benefit from this event.

The only way we were going to get a president to understand all of the issues that we had all been working on for years was to get all the candidates in the same place, at the same time, so that they could understand what we are faced with on a daily basis. With the help of these groups, I developed a coalition of people to sponsor a forum right here in South Carolina. Though they were initially skeptical, they saw enough of the big picture to work toward materializing the vision.

After the picture was painted, the entire community came on board because they all saw themselves as part of the picture—they all represented a part of the whole. However, at this juncture, we were unable to get any presidential candidate to commit. We also did not have the financial means to pull off this event. We were a small, grassroots group, and we estimated that it would take approximately $500,000 to host the forum. Realizing our limitations, we sought the assistance of a Washington, D.C.-based organization that was trying to hold the candidates accountable for the same issues, but they sought to do so through policy discussions. I approached them by saying, "What if we gave you a venue to cosponsor an event with some grassroots organizations that would guarantee that all presidential candidates would be there? We'll turn out a number of people, and you can do the same to make this event an American forum." They thought this was an excellent idea because they wanted an opportunity to get face-to face with the candidates. They agreed to cover the costs of the venue and hire their media staff to film the event.

Approximately forty grassroots groups and forty nationwide groups committed to being present at the event; however, at this point we still did not have any commitment from the presidential candidates. So we employed a strategy to force the candidates to believe that if they did not show up, there was no possible way they would win the presidency. And just as I had painted the big picture for my peers and countless organizations, I proceeded to paint the big picture for the presidential candidates. I let them know there would be an audience of 3,000 voters, and there was no other place, before the presidential primaries, that they would find an audience of 3,000 voters—and whoever did the best at this event would more than likely win the presidency. Soon after painting this picture, Al Sharpton and Dennis Kucinich committed. Then, after conducting some research, I learned that a friend of mine working for Wesley Clark's campaign was willing to speak to his camp on my behalf. As favor would have it, Clark's camp was slated to be in Greenville, South Carolina, two days before the forum, and they agreed to extend their stay to participate in our event. After receiving Wesley Clark's commitment, I informed all the other candidates that Clark was confirmed and he would be given an entire hour of airtime (on WIS-TV, which covered nearly every county of South Carolina in its viewing area) to present his stance if they did not show. Soon after, Howard Dean, John Edwards, and John Kerry all committed to attending the event. Consequently, they unknowingly bought into the vision and, in doing so, brought it to fruition.

On January 30, 2004, we had an auditorium full of 3,200 people, with three hundred news/media outlets that covered the event, which was broadcast live nationwide and in various parts of the world. The event was called "The People's Agenda for Economic Justice: A Dialogue with America's Families." Representatives from approximately every state were present. Instead of having the candidates conduct a forum amongst themselves, where they pontificated and debated, we used grassroots leaders to pose real-life issues. The candidates were brought out one by one, then they were given two minutes to state how they planned on ending poverty in America; thereafter, they answered questions from the grassroots leaders under the direction of Tom Joyner, the host of a self-titled nationally syndicated morning radio show, who was our moderator.

This was the first time, since 1964, that a presidential candidate directly addressed poverty in America. This was the first time since then that any candidate actually said they would end poverty in America; Howard Dean said, "If you vote for me, I will end child poverty in ten years, and this is how I plan on doing it ..." The picture was painted, the vision was ignited, and as a result, the mission was accomplished. This event all started with a vision—my vision, which was birthed from the need for government officials to address poverty in America, and this vision ultimately materialized into a successful presidential forum. Hence, where there is vision, there is the potential for action, and where there is action, there is progress.

"Your own resolution to success is more important than any other one thing."

- Abraham Lincoln

CHAPTER THREE

ESSENTIAL NUMBER 2: HAVE COMMITMENT

The second quality that is important for transformative leadership in the twenty-first century is *commitment*. Throughout the last century, it became very difficult to find leaders who would remain committed to any one cause. Instead, many of them were part-time leaders. These so-called leaders move aimlessly from cause to cause, organization to organization, and community to community. In the process of moving around, they never really help their organization achieve their goals. This lack of commitment is equivalent to an athlete working enough to say they played in the game, but not hard enough to win the game. This kind of mentality is bad for successful sports teams, and it is even worse for someone in leadership. Failing to see your cause through from start to finish is nothing short of quitting. It is difficult to ensure success when those who are supposed to follow you often see leaders who willingly quit easily. People want leaders who will not quit. The public needs leaders who are willing to stay and fight for their vision to become a reality.

Transformative leadership requires that one has the audacity to stay focused on reaching the goal long after the feeling and excitement of setting that goal has left that leader. Commitment also compels a leader to stand up in the face of adversity to ensure success. It is most important to stay strong during adversity. In any leadership task, there will always be opposition. If you are boldly leading your group, organization, or community into uncharted territory, there will be some doubt about success. There will be some pain, fear, and concern about failure. At each hurdle, a leader will be forced to make a decision. We will always be forced to choose. At this point, we must ask ourselves, Will I let this obstacle stop me, or will I continue toward the vision that I've set for my organization? Making the choice to continue to live out the vision is evidence of true commitment.

When a leader has commitment, he or she is willing to demonstrate it to all levels of the leadership hierarchy. First, a leader must demonstrate commitment to the vision. Second, a leader must demonstrate commitment to the change process. Next, commitment must be demonstrated to the organization. Finally, and most importantly, commitment must be demonstrated to the people who help make the transformative change. To call yourself a committed, visionary leader, you must be willing to submit yourself to all phases of the organization's leadership hierarchy: the vision, the process, the organization, and the people. And, after seeing the project through, a leader must be willing to commit to accepting the expected and unexpected changes that come with transformation. In essence, transformative leaders are determined to see their project through from start to finish—regardless of the challenges, or changes. They remain committed, no matter what the outcome.

Another key phase of the commitment process that all twenty-first-century leaders must master is personal self-improvement. A leader must understand why it is important to become a better leader. It must be your goal to recognize that you are never your best—there is always room for improvement. The internal commitment to always do more will always put you in a better position for success. There is always more that we can do to become better leaders. Staying focused on your path will change the dynamic within any organization, group, church, or community. When the people know they have a leader who has an unwavering commitment to being a better leader, their confidence in that leader will increase dramatically.

In order to gain understanding on how to become a committed leader, you must embrace the four P's of commitment: purpose, passion, power, and persistence. The first P stands for *Purpose*. You must have a purpose for why you are seeking to be a transformative leader. To know your purpose, a set of questions must be asked: What do you hope to gain from being a leader? Who do you hope to help as a leader? What problem do you hope to solve? What success do you want to create? Why you? Why now? You must know the reasons why. You must define why you want to be a leader. You must be able to explain what motivates you to get up every single day and work toward your goals. You must know your purpose for leadership by understanding why you are doing this. Understanding why helps you to understand the process of what you must commit to do to obtain audacious leadership status.

The second P is for *Passion*. You must be passionate about your cause, company, community, or organization. If you do not have passion for your mission, you will not be able to commit to what you need to do. Passion is very important for transformative leadership. Passion is what will inspire others to continue to follow you during adversity. There is an old saying in the community organizing field that says, "People do not care what you know, until they know that you care"—having passion shows that you care. Knowing and showing that you care reinforces your ability to become a transformative, *audacious leader*. You must be passionate about your purpose. You cannot be afraid to speak from your heart. You cannot be afraid to let your heart lead you toward your purpose.

The third P in commitment is for *Power*. Power is the confidence that you have all the knowledge necessary to lead people to a greater future. To master your power in commitment, you must arm yourself with the knowledge and information that it takes to become a great leader. Knowing what it takes to become a great leader can be obtained by reading this book, and any other materials that prepare you for your leadership endeavors. Once you know what it takes to become a great leader and you're confident in the process of leadership, you will have unfettered direction toward becoming a committed leader.

The fourth P is for *Persistence*—you must have the mentality that you will never give up, never give in, and never quit. You must persistently challenge yourself to be a great leader. You must persistently work to express your vision, your passion, and your purpose to be a great leader. You must not settle for second best or the word "no." Persistence is working to make the impossible, possible. It can also be seen as exhausting all possibilities. By having this level of persistence, you will set yourself apart from other leaders.

Mastering the four P's for commitment will help to develop audacious leadership within you. As a committed leader, you will exude purpose, passion, power, and persistence, and these qualities at work will produce success.

Whether you believe this or not, the basic purpose of having commitment in leadership is to help those leaders who will follow you. The people who follow you will do what you do. If they see you waver in your commitment, they too will waver in the work that they are willing to put toward your vision and your organizational goals. As a transformative leader, you must provide an example of committed leadership. Leadership creates for them a never-ending example of working toward the goal of the vision. As the leader, you must demonstrate your commitment in order for the people to have confidence in you and your vision.

The first step to putting commitment to action is to have a set of values and beliefs to validate your involvement in leadership. These underlying values will define your uniqueness and the direction in which you want to take your organization, church, or group. Having the commitment of underlying values will lead you toward a unifying vision and the purpose within your organization. It will also keep you from straying from your mission as a leader.

After establishing a set of values that undergird your level of commitment, you must display a strong sense of personal integrity and self-confidence that is beyond reproach. No one should ever question your commitment to the group. People in your world should not have to question your veracity. They should never question your willingness to be held accountable or hold other people accountable. People should never have to question whether you will do the right thing. As a leader, you must remain true to the vision and honest with the people involved.

The second step to putting commitment in action is to create a leadership plan. There is an old saying used in community organizing: "If you fail to plan, then you plan to fail." This saying about planning is critical to your commitment. This plan must consist of daily tasks that you will do to reinforce your commitment, and make it a daily routine. This routine is what I call a Daily Method of Operation (DMO). Your DMO is a checklist of what you must do to get better as a leader and to reinforce to your organization that they should continue to follow you. Never take for granted that people should follow you. Each day, you have to give them another reason why they should continue to follow you. These new reasons are what you do in your DMO.

The story of Napoleon Bonaparte's rise to leadership in the French army is one of legend.[5] Napoleon was a fierce leader and fighter. He was also an incredibly successful motivator of his troops because he continued to demonstrate his commitment.

As a general in the French army, Napoleon was able to successfully motivate soldiers to fight battles on his behalf because of his personal commitment to participating in the battle. During many battles, when his troops were tired and beaten, Napoleon wanted to make sure his army understood his level of commitment. As a leader and a commander, he committed himself to the offensive by getting off of his horse and going out to fight on the front line of the battlefield. In many instances, Napoleon would be more aggressive on the front lines than his men who were following his leadership. Napoleon even received life-threatening injuries as he fought these battles. One injury was a bayonet to the thigh. Nonetheless, his demonstrated commitment to his troops won him many battles, but it also reinforced his leadership abilities to leaders in France. Those French leaders rewarded Napoleon's commitment by placing him in charge of the army.

It was Napoleon's goal to show his troops and the French leaders that he possessed authority, that he was a military genius, and that he had the ability to help France conquer the world. He displayed this purpose in his passion to be up for the fight. He would constantly run from the rear of his army and take the lead of his troops across the battlefield. He would be the first into battle and put himself in harm's way before his troops were in harm's way. This demonstrated his passionate approach to military leadership. Napoleon demonstrated his power to his French leaders by being successful in every battle that he was in charge of. He was always willing to demonstrate his military power. Napoleon's ability to bring military success to any battle was due to his persistence that his leadership and planning was the best.

In 1996, I had been working at the South Carolina Fair Share for about six months as a community organizer. I was extremely excited about being a grassroots leader. I got up every day thrilled that I would be earning a paycheck to organize communities toward their goals. I felt like I was doing a good job and this was something that I could enjoy doing for a long time. The only problem was it clearly didn't pay enough. My $18,500 annual salary, for working fifty hours a week, was not enough to pay my bills. Nonetheless, I enjoyed working to bring community visions to reality.

One day, my supervisor came to me and said that she was going to have to let me go. The grant money that was providing my salary had run out. She told me that I was good at the work but being the newest hire, I would be the first to go. I was devastated by this information. I loved my job. I loved getting paid, even though my paycheck was very small. I felt like what I was doing was valuable. It was making a difference in people's lives by addressing the need to improve access to affordable health care in our community. I had built a team of community leaders who were excited about working with me and felt that I was leading them in the right direction.

After being laid off, I thought, "What would happen to the people in the community that were depending on me to show up? Would they think that I gave up on them, their community, and the issues they cared about? If I stopped coming to the meetings because I couldn't get paid to do so, would they think I was only in it for the money?" I was devastated about losing my paycheck but I was even more devastated that I would not be there to work on the issues the community cared about. Since I believed so strongly in the work of bringing people together, even after being told by my boss that I was being laid off, I made a decision to keep working without a paycheck, indefinitely.

I ultimately felt that there was a higher purpose at work. The need to work to improve the quality of the lives of poverty-stricken families became more important than making money to pay my bills. I understood clearly that there would be no financial gain or reward by continuing to work on the community health care reform efforts. However, I firmly believed that staying committed to the people, informing them about their rights, and empowering them to undertake efforts that would improve their health care was more important than anything that would happen to me. I was committed to this cause, no matter what.

During this time period, I became more immersed in my work of understanding health policy and community organizing. I literally forgot about myself and concentrated on being the best organizer and advocate I could be. I worked aggressively to fulfill the vision of South Carolina Fair Share. In fact, I seemingly worked harder without earning a paycheck than I did while I was earning a paycheck. It was during this time of working for free that my unending commitment began to pay me back by elevating my leadership.

My supervisor watched my work ethic and efforts during this time period. She knew that she could not require me to work without compensation, but she saw me show up for work every day. It was in these days of my selfless work for grassroots people that my boss began to significantly appreciate my commitment and my service to the organization and the people we represented. She worked aggressively to raise revenues to restore me to full-time employee status. After several weeks of selflessly committing to improve our health care system as a "volunteer", I was restored to full-time employment.

My loyalty and commitment were greatly appreciated by my supervisor, so much so that she offered to assist me in finding a better job because she now believed that I deserved a greater leadership role in nonprofit sector. She offered to help me to find a better job so that I could play a bigger role in community work. I was shocked that my boss offered to help me find another job. In fact, I thought that she didn't like my work during the time I was a non-paid employee. However, I later discovered this was not the case; she was very happy with my work and believed that I deserved to earn more than what she could afford to pay me. She believed that I deserved to lead at a higher level, where I would be able to impact more lives.

My level of demonstrated commitment influenced my current employer to help me find better employment. And finding better employment is exactly what she did for me. She assisted me in getting a job that nearly doubled my previous salary. This new employment increased my responsibilities beyond what I could have imagined. I went from doing work in two small local communities to doing work across the state of South Carolina. This gave me greater experience that helped shape my vision for how leadership can improve our state. It was only because of my commitment that I gained this new opportunity for leadership.

"Honesty is the cornerstone of all success, without which confidence and ability to perform shall cease to exist."

-Mary Kay Ash, Founder of Mary Kay Cosmetics

CHAPTER FOUR

ESSENTIAL NUMBER 3: BE AUTHENTIC

Transformative leaders must possess authenticity in all of their endeavors. People will follow authenticity, whether it is good or bad. There is a reason why in movies, and in real life, it is easy to see "the bad guys" rise to power. They keep it real—they are unabashedly honest about their intentions and their actions. On the other hand, there are some "good guy" leaders who try to be everything to everyone. Instead of just being themselves, they appear pretentious. But keeping it real and truthful (particularly during adversity) enhances your leadership and credibility.

Over the last two decades, we have grown accustomed to choosing leaders because of their style rather than their substance. I remember during the 2004 and 2008 presidential primary elections, many local pundits and political insiders discussed the qualities of who they thought should be the next president of the United States. They would limitedly discuss the individual's résumé and background. But they would spend most of their energy talking about "who *looked* more presidential." It concerned me that people were looking for a leader who *looked like* he or she could win, rather than one who had the ability to win. We also wanted a leader who *looked like* he or she could run the country, rather than one who actually had the temperament to run the country. As Americans, we have been engrossed with the idea of style in our leaders. While it is important to have a unique flavor (style) in presenting yourself as a leader, style becomes a problem when you make it more important than the content of your character. We often are guilty of choosing style over substance by focusing on questions like, who looks like a leader? Who dresses like a leader? Who stands like a leader? Who sounds like a leader? In doing so, we neglect to ask the questions that address the substance of the matter, which are, Who knows what it takes to be a real leader? Who has the experience that is needed to be a real leader?

AUTHENTICITY IN LEADERSHIP

Audacious leadership in the twenty-first century requires you to make leadership about substance. This means that you must have complete authenticity. Leadership must reflect the content of your character not just the image that you want to project. Your image is your style, but your character is what gives you substances as a leader. You have to be focused on sharing with the world the authentic substance within you that gives you the audacity to lead. Authentic substance is defined as being honest, genuine, or real, and this is what's missing from leadership today. Some leaders in the twenty-first century struggle with keeping it real. Instead of honesty, they present fabricated ideas about who they are, what their experiences are, and where they stand. In this era of public relations messaging and branding, it is easy to only learn about what people want you to know about them, versus who they really are. All you have to do is look at the exposure of former presidential candidate John Edwards, former Enron CEO Ken Lay, former AIG CEO Martin Sullivan, Pastor Ted Haggard, former Congressman Tom Foley, and former Senator Larry Craig. All of these men were in leadership positions, or seeking leadership in the highest levels of our country, and in the process of doing so, their secret habits were exposed. They were not completely honest. To be a great leader, you must always keep it real—be true to yourself and be honest to those with whom you interact. Being yourself matters more than anything else. Bold leaders will let themselves be defined by the character they possess and the experiences that have shaped their lives. Authenticity is especially important when situations get difficult. When there is struggle, strife, or hard times in your life, who you really are (your character), will always overshadow your image. In the face of adversity, many people resort to letting their guard down, and if you are not authentic, people will see behind your facade and know how you really are. The truth always comes out. On the contrary, if you practice authenticity, you will not be easily shaken, and the people will be glad you maintained a consistent character through any crisis.

THE IMPORTANCE OF AUTHENTICITY

Keeping it real is important because it allows those that follow you to identify with your personal human experience. Your supporters need to be able to see you as a real person. They need to see someone who has shared life experiences that are similar to their own. Supporters need to witness the complexity of humanity within you. All of those complexities and characteristics give your supporters an opportunity to identify in themselves those characteristics that are most like you. If they have no idea who the real you is, all that you actually stand for, and all that you believe in, it will be difficult for them to understand your purpose. They will also find it hard to grasp why they should consider following you. Being authentic allows people to connect with your leadership and follow the model of leadership that you set. As we will see in later chapters, the strength of your leadership will be measured by the lasting effect you have on people. Authentic leaders will always have a lasting effect because of their ability to draw others of shared backgrounds to their experiences. People are not just drawn to causes; they are drawn to leaders they believe in—leaders who happen to champion some causes.

The initial step to becoming an authentic leader is being able to tell your story. Telling your story is the most important part of practicing authentic leadership. People have to understand where you came from, as well as your life's experiences, to see what has made you the person you are today. You have to be willing to share those experiences with those who follow you (directly and indirectly).

In the previous chapters, we discussed why vision and commitment are important to establish a foundation for leadership. Vision and commitment show others where and how to plan to lead. Now you need to show authenticity to express why you want to lead and why you should lead. To tap into and express your authenticity to those that you hope will follow you, you must be able to share your *whys*. You must be able to tell your story. Why are you here? Why now? What life experiences brought you to this effort? Which encounter in your life brought you to seek leadership? Never be afraid to tell anyone who you are and why you do what you do. Your story should include what has made you successful. Focus on your personal strengthens and the opportunities you were given. It should also include your weaknesses and your fears. Your story is the complete picture of how you have become a leader.

In the era of style over substance, most people do not recognize how valuable their personal stories can be to someone else's experience. There is a lot that can be learned from other people involved in a situation that can give hope and inspiration to others who have not yet reached their potential in leadership. Your story can motivate someone to keep going when he or she is on the verge of quitting. Your story can inspire others to action. Your experience can give confidence to other leaders.

Sharing your story is rather humbling, and contrary to what others will tell you, it does not highlight your weaknesses. Instead, revealing your story shows your increased strength and ability to talk about your vulnerable moments—it ultimately reveals that you've used your obstacles in life as a stepping-stone into leadership. Your story matters in everything that you hope to accomplish. Leaders should never be afraid to tell the story of where they came from, because they realize that their past is directly connected to the person that they are today. The purpose of telling your story is to give others a clear idea of the values and experiences that have brought you to your organization or group and, hopefully, motivate others to tap into their own leadership abilities. There is no greater motivator for personal achievement than hearing from someone who has your same values and experiences that caused them to become a leader.

The second characteristic of authentic leaders is that they do not run from their mistakes. If you make a mistake, you should be the first to admit it. Along with admitting that a mistake was made, you should be prepared to share what you have learned from that experience. Again, in the era of style versus substance, and branding and messaging over truth, rarely do leaders willingly own up to their shortcomings. Think about the experience we had with former President Bill Clinton and his affair with Monica Lewinsky; he was afraid to admit he made a mistake, and his dishonesty ultimately tainted his reputation in the public's eye. Likewise, leaders of Enron, Tyco, and WorldCom as well as convicted investment manager Bernard Madoff all refused to tell the truth and admit their mistakes, and their disloyalty tainted the American people's view of good corporate leadership. But there is one thing that has held true for the American people—we are a people of second chances. If leaders own up to their mistakes and talk about what they have learned from them, they can be redeemed to leadership status. So to be a transformative leader in the twenty-first century, we must get back to admitting our mistakes so that we can become better leaders.

In addition to admitting their mistakes, transformative leaders should be willing to take ownership of their opportunities. You should take ownership of opportunities that are good and bad. Individuals born into this world are not responsible for how they are born, nor are they responsible for where they are born. Individuals are not responsible for how their parents chose to raise them. But we are responsible for how we conduct ourselves in the present and the future. Being an authentic, transformative leader requires you to take ownership of your present and the future. As you will learn in later chapters, leaders must take action to own their future. This means you must use all you have learned and all that you have been given to work toward a better world community.

The third characteristic that an authentic leader must exemplify is one of transparency. We must have leaders who can operate in transparency. They must never be afraid to show others how they accomplish their goals and objectives. I know it is sometimes hard to open up your work ethic to public scrutiny. The fear of sharing how we make progress in our lives can leave us all feeling very vulnerable. It might even give you the sense that somehow, by being transparent, you are compromising your formula for success in life. But in light of the current state of our political, corporate, and religious leadership, being transparent is more important to restore confidence in our institutions of leadership than anything you may lose from being transparent. Transformative leaders must restore the confidence of the public in our leaders.

In addition to being transparent, as a transformative leader you must practice stewardship—you must be responsible and accountable for all of the leadership power that you are given. You must not squander your opportunities—instead, you should maximize them to help others. If you gain wealth because of your leadership position, you must give more wealth back to others who are less fortunate. If you gain power and other resources in your position, then you must leave more than you gained; in doing so, you will foster a reciprocal pattern and practice of good stewardship that will have a long-lasting impact on the people that you serve. If you are real and giving to the people that you lead, they will also be real and giving to others that they may lead.

When President Barack Obama penned his autobiography *Dreams from My Father,*[6] it was an open and honest story of a biracial child's understanding of what race meant in his life. In this expressive story, he shared that his growth and development as a man was impacted by the places he lived, the people he lived with, and the experiences that changed his outlook on life. He also talked about the struggles of his biracial identity as a teenager. He talked about how those struggles led him at one time to use drugs. He was the first African American president of the *Harvard Law Review,* but as a leader he told the unadulterated truth about who he was as a person and how he would continue to operate as a leader. This book was incredibly revealing about the person we know as Barack Obama. It was an honest assessment of who he was and is; what he valued and experienced; and what he expected people to know about him. This book also was a revealing story about his life and upbringing that drove him to become a leader in helping poor neighborhoods solve their problems. The book revealed what drove Barack Obama to become a community organizer.

Dreams from My Father gave everyone in America the ability to see who Barack Obama truly is as a person. If you really want to learn how Barack Obama thinks, what he values, what he cares about, and what information he uses to make decisions, you can find this analysis in *Dreams from My Father.* It was one of the most revealing books ever by anyone who sought to become the leader of the free world. Other presidents have written the story of their leadership after they completed their term in public office, but not before. These leaders seemed to be hesitant to talk about their transformative experiences because of the vulnerabilities that these expressions would create. On the contrary, Barack Obama has shared his vulnerabilities with those before his leadership, and it helped to inform us more about why he wanted to lead. Even for me, his ability to share his weaknesses helped me relate to him. By sharing his weaknesses, it helped others relate to him. He also explained how those weaknesses were the inspiration to do greater things for our world community.

As I have grown to become a community-focused political leader in South Carolina, I have always been asked why I wanted to get involved in politics and what motivated me to want to change lives and improve communities? Each time I am asked these questions, I give the same answer: "Hip hop music." Yes, hip hop music and culture are what motivated me to get involved in the community and politics.

It all started when I was a mischievous adolescent in Norfolk, Virginia. In the mid-1980s, many of the inner-city summer camps, after-school programs, and recreation programs began cutting back on activities they provided for preteens and teens. Even my favorite summer camp program hosted by the Urban League disappeared. Several of my childhood friends never even had camps or programs in their neighborhoods. We had very few productive activities in our community. The few programs we had were sometimes too far from our neighborhoods for most of us to attend, which left us all to hang out on the street corners after school with older kids. Some of them had been in jail at least once; others were one caper away from going to jail. Nonetheless, I was intrigued by their rough lifestyles and their willingness to rebel against the system. I began spending more time on the corners and the parks with them than I spent pursuing productive activities. I didn't want to play football or basketball. I just wanted to hang out with the rough crowd. Soon, I began to get peer pressured to participate in mischievous, and oftentimes illegal, activities. Unfortunately, for the next year, I hung out with this crew daily after school, with nothing to do but create trouble. Some of our favorite pastimes were skipping school and drinking booze from a parent's liquor cabinet or petty shoplifting from convenience stores. Eventually, our mischievous habits landed us in serious trouble.

I was fourteen years old when my friends and I were joyriding around in a stolen car. I was in the back of the car, and my two older friends (sixteen and seventeen) were in the front. Before I knew what was happening, there were red and blue lights flashing behind us. Rather than pulling over and owning up to what we had done, my friends decided to try and escape the police. This turned into a high-speed chase. The driver headed toward a cemetery in our city that bordered on a small wooded area. On most days, these woods were a sanctuary for us. We frequently hung out there to drink and curse while playing hooky from school. But on this day, we hoped these woods would serve as a refuge to escape police custody. My friend stopped the car by the cemetery, and we all tried to get out, making a mad dash to the woods through the cemetery. But my growing body was crammed into the backseat of a two-seater, and I got hung up in the front seat's seatbelt while trying to jump out. So the police grabbed me and caught up with both of my friends. In that moment, we realized we were undoubtedly headed to jail.

When we arrived in the station, they separated us into different rooms. The typical police tactic is to get to the bottom of the story by interrogating the youngest juvenile first. And I was prepared to come clean and face the consequences of my actions. Before I could talk with the officers and confess what we had done, I learned that one of my friends took the entire blame for our crime. He told the cops that he had stolen the car without my knowledge, and that I had just come for the ride. Soon after his confession, the police came to me and told me that they had the full story, and I should stop hanging with bad kids before I got into serious trouble. They then said, "You're free to go home." That day, I walked out of the police station a free teenager, knowing that I should have taken the fall for my actions.

After getting questioned by the police, and escaping a situation that could have landed me in some serious trouble, I decided to walk back home rather than catching the city bus. As I was walking for several miles, I came upon a local shopping center that my friends and I frequented as our local hangout spot. I noticed the local radio station truck parked outside of the music store. The truck caught my attention, so I stopped in the music store to see what new rap music they were promoting. At this time, hip hop and rap music was a growing art form, but was largely unknown to most people over twenty-five years old. It was popular to youth my age, and it wasn't unusual for us to spend hours at a time in record stores. Once inside, I went to the new music rack to look for the latest rap albums. One album cover in particular caught my eye; in fact, I stared at it intensely because it reminded me of my recent encounter with the police. It had a picture of two men in a prison cell. The photograph of these two men behind bars spoke to me. I was amazed at the imagery and wondered why they were in a jail cell. I desperately wanted to know what kind of hip hop this was, so I quickly purchased this rap album on cassette tape. That tape was Public Enemy's *It Takes a Nation of Millions to Hold Us Back.* I wanted to know why this group called themselves "Public Enemy"; was it because they were dangerous? Who was after them? Did they make this album from inside a prison cell? As I began listening to their music, my first education on leadership began.

Public Enemy was not a traditional rap group of the era. Most groups at the time began making records to gain wealth and fame with their music. This was not the case with Public Enemy. When they signed their first record contract, Chuck D, the leader of Public Enemy, stated that one of their goals in music was to inspire and create 5,000 new black community leaders by the end of that record contract. As a part of this goal, Public Enemy sought to educate youth through their music. Public Enemy's music spoke politically about the social issues impacting urban, African American communities. They rapped about the problems with drug addiction, unemployment, crime, police brutality, failed community leadership, and racism. Their music was designed to invoke frustration and outrage at these problems, as well as inspire young people to do something about these problems. Their music expressed the sense that because of poor public policy and the ignorance of what happens to people in underserved communities that America was creating a vicious cycle of social problems. The music expressed that we must do something about these problems. I heard their message loud and clear. As an urban teen in America, I was subject to become a victim of all of those social ills they addressed. Each day was another chance that I could get caught up in the criminal justice system or the vicious cycle of poverty.

Their music encouraged me to protect myself from these social ills by arming myself with a lethal weapon. However, the lethal weapon Public Enemy referred to was not a knife or a gun, as you may suppose. Instead, the lethal weapon I needed to possess was *an educated mind.* They taught me that it was my responsibility to rise above the image that some would associate with my youth and my black skin. Their music spoke to my core and taught me to arm myself with knowledge, because knowledge was the key to power and leadership that could ultimately bring about positive change.

They taught me that knowledge was the power that I needed to develop leadership skills to change social ills in America. Knowledge was also the power that could never be taken away from me. Through their music, I learned self-respect, self-awareness, and discipline, and most importantly, I learned how to be socially conscious. The music inspired me to pay attention to issues in our communities. The drugs, crime, and poverty were part of the focus. The music inspired me to read and learn how I could help deal with these problems. The music taught me how poor communities could avoid self-destruction.

Chuck D and Public Enemy became role models for many through their music. They inspired me to learn about my world as it is and how to work to make the world what it should be. Because of Public Enemy and other positive hip hop artists of that era, my knowledge reigned supreme over nearly everyone my age. Public Enemy was a cut against the grain of party songs and the braggadocio in the music industry at that time. Everyone else made celebratory songs and party music. However, their music was serious and thought provoking. They *kept it real* (hip hop slang for being honest and truthful) and told people like me what we needed to hear, not what we wanted to hear. Public Enemy's goal was to educate and inspire young people to be community leaders, and after hearing this album, I was convinced that I would become one. To this day, I believe that education, commitment, and service are essential to community improvement—these qualities are essential to leadership. This music group's influence caused me to develop an addiction to learning about how to become a better person. This addiction to learning was critical to my leadership development. And learning, as we will address later, is essential to transformative leadership.

Public Enemy's music served as a convicting sermon that changed my worldview. Consequently, I quit hanging out on the streets with the older kids, and I chose to associate with people my own age, who shared my interests. I stayed home to read more and listen to more positive rap music. When I was not reading, I was listening to rap. If I wasn't doing either of those things, I was rapping Public Enemy's lyrics with my friends. And as a result, I became one of the 5,000 leaders that Public Enemy commissioned in their music.

While some may frown upon my poor decisions as an adolescent, those experiences helped to change my life. The bad experience of being in a police station propelled me into an opposite direction. I learned that putting myself in those kinds of situations, hanging with those kinds of people, would lead me to self-destruction. And Public Enemy shared through their music why taking pride in yourself was important and taking ownership for the problems in your community was even more important. I also learned that we needed leaders to take ownership of both the problems and the communities. I was inspired toward this ownership by their music. I was inspired to take action in my community. I was inspired to be a leader in this changing world. It was hip hop that helped shape me. Hip hop focused me on what happens to people in poor communities. Hip hop inspired me to be a leader in everything I did from that point going forward.

It is through hip hop music that I learned about social problems and how our political systems are connected to solving these problems. It is my experience of going on the wrong path of theft, drinking and smoking as a teen that motivates me every day to do the right things and to live as honorably as I can. It is because of these experiences that I understand my role as a leader. So you should never be afraid to be transparent. Always tell people what they need to hear, rather than what they want to hear. And strive to encourage people to be who they really are, as well as know the reasons for the things they do.

"The ear of the leader must ring with the voices of the people."

-Woodrow Wilson

CHAPTER FIVE

Essential Number 4: Learn to Listen

It seems that the world has lost the art of listening. In doing so, we have become self-centered and insular individuals. We are consumed with listening to what is important to ourselves, rather than what's important to others. Leaders are also apt to ignore the voices of those around them. Listening is a skill that has become a lost art for leaders. They tend not to listen to those who follow and support them. Many of them believe that because they are the leaders, they don't have to value what other people say. They also think that they have been innately gifted with all the knowledge, skills, ideas, and abilities that it takes to lead. But to be a transformative leader in the twenty-first century, you must know that you don't know everything. You should have confidence in your abilities, but you should also be willing to humbly open yourself up to gain knowledge from others who are not in a leadership position. Gaining newfound knowledge requires you to listen.

In addition to listening, it is a leader's responsibility to be a messenger in this world. The role of the messenger is vital. It is vital to help others understand important concepts as they relate to your organization or group. Some leaders cannot help others to understand these important concepts because the leader has lost the ability to hone in on what's important to those on the front lines of our organizations, businesses, and communities. Some leaders have chosen not to listen to the concerns of the people. When we don't listen, we oftentimes lead people in the wrong direction because we (the messengers) become disconnected from the realities of those on the front lines. People generally expect a leader to take them to new heights, but they also expect a leader to be connected to the reality of where they have come from. So a leader must be willing listen and learn from the experiences of their supporters. The people who support you can provide valuable insight that will help you lead them in the right direction. Their input will enable you to be a better advocate. However, if the leader is disconnected and does not listen, some problems and issues can remain unresolved, and those same problems could potentially derail your support for your vision. Hence, it is the leader's responsibility to both listen and relay the voiced needs of the people within his or her organization.

To be a transformative leader in the twenty-first century, you must master the art of listening. Listening requires the hearer to get out of his or her own life and put on the shoes of another human being. You must be willing to listen to the people you want to lead. Listening is the process of building trust and understanding to communicate ideas across the social spectrum; it is the power to hear people's words and understand exactly what their words mean; it is finding out what's important to those you come in contact with. For transformative leaders, listening is about relating to people.

Listening gives you the opportunity to learn more so that you can lead others in the right direction. I believe there is a reason why God created man with two ears and one mouth. We should do twice as much listening as we do speaking. When we listen, we can learn much more information and better our leadership skills to positively impact the people we lead.

Listening sets a foundation to build long-term commitment with those that you (the leader) serve. It requires you to focus your attention on those who are helping you to grow in your leadership position. Listening compels you to understand where your vision needs to grow and how to make it more inclusive, how it is to respond to adversity, and how to make sure that you do not go in the wrong direction.

Having a keen sense to listen to those who follow you, is critical to transformative leadership. You have to take time to listen to your followers. You have to take time to listen to the information that could help you become a better leader—by doing so, both you and the people you lead will benefit.

Listening to others helps to mold and shape our leadership skills. If we choose not to listen, we are likely destined to face unnecessary hardship, because we did not take the time to learn the right from the wrong. However, we can spare ourselves these mistakes by learning from the wisdom of others. Solomon of the Bible once said, "Listen, my child, to what your father teaches you. Don't neglect your mother's teaching"[7] In other words, we can learn from our parents, friends, and everyone they were connected to, but the learning only comes through listening. We have to be willing to listen to how they coped with the challenges they faced in their own lives. We may not face the exact same challenges, but it may be helpful to know that we are not the only ones facing opposition. Knowledge and understanding can be gained from every conversation you have with another person. Your direct and indirect interaction with others will afford you wisdom.

So, as a transformative leader of the twenty-first century, you should ask, what can I learn from this conversation and what should I do with the information I have heard today? Once you have received an answer to these questions, you must actively apply the information and knowledge you have gained to your leadership endeavors.

LEARNING TO BE A TRANSFORMATIVE LISTENER

Becoming an effective transformative leader requires you to build relationships with others. In our dog-eat-dog world, one of the greatest gifts given to a human being is the ability to sit and listen to someone. As a leader, you must be willing to get to know the people within your group, church, organization, or business. You have to get to know the people that you are working with to learn the pressing issues in their lives.

To begin this process, you have to allow people to tell their stories. Just as you would share your story to show them your audacious pursuit of leadership, you have to allow them to tell the story of why they are involved in your efforts. This may be very hard to do in our eight-second-sound-bite world. News programs, debates, commercials, public service announcements, and text messages have made us all learn to listen and speak in sound bites. This method of listening doesn't allow any of us to get the context surrounding an issue—very little is learned in eight seconds. Sound-bite communication may be good for marketing, and for twenty-four-hour news cycles, but it destroys your ability to become a transformative leader. We have to work past these communicative limitations.

An effective transformative leader masters the art of helping people to tell their stories, in order to create the space for you to hear their spoken and unspoken issues. We must ask questions that relate to the positives and negatives in any given situation. You should be clear that your interest is to help them achieve their goals and dreams. You are asking to learn what you can do to make their goals and dreams possible. You must truly show your interest in them. Your questions should create an atmosphere of shared learning. Ultimately, your goal is to uncover their *perceived reality*.

Communication is broken down into two parts. Communication is 10 percent words and 90 percent body language and tone. When you listen, you should tune in 100 percent. You should ask yourself, What parts of the story are left out; are there obvious holes in what is presented; what does their body language tell me about this story; are they uncomfortable; is the story painful to tell; are their facial expressions animated; are they passionately excited about telling their story?

After listening carefully, you should repeat and verify what has been said (and what has not been said). In doing so, you will be able to voice your understanding of what was said directly and indirectly to make a holistic conclusion. Transformative leaders must get clarification to avoid making assumptions and presumptions. You should have a clear understanding of what the people want and what they need. Never assume you already know.

By gaining clarity from the people, you will be able to map out the direction you should take as a leader. You should be certain that your intended path is relevant and beneficial to the people you are trying to serve. You must connect the dots between your plans and the concerns of the people. And you must make certain that all parties (other leaders and your supporters) have a clear understanding and connection to the vision, or the bigger picture.

Active and intentional listening for twenty-first-century leaders demands that you are aware of the things that are bigger than you and bigger than anyone's particular situation. When someone says something to you about your leadership or your organization, you must be able to hear all the issues within the comment. You should then take that information and translate it to the people within your organization to address the concerns at hand. By articulating the real problem, together you can address it. This ensures that you and your group can continue to pursue your purpose. Ultimately, transformative leaders are active and intentional listeners who are grounded in the realities of the people they serve. So by listening, you will keep people engaged and committed to the vision.

EXAMPLE FROM A TRANSFORMATIVE LEADER

Robert F. Kennedy created an opportunity to listen. In April of 1967, he and Charles Evers traveled to the Mississippi Delta to see the poverty that existed there. He was struck to the core by what he was listening to.

> Kennedy sees a small child with a swollen stomach sitting in the corner. He tries and tries to talk to this child again and again, but he gets no response, no movement, not even a look of awareness. Just a blank stare from cold, wide eyes so battered by poverty that they're barely alive.

> And at that point we're told that Kennedy begins to cry. And he turns to Evers and asks, "How can a country like this allow it?" and Evers responds, "Maybe they just don't know."[8]

But Robert F. Kennedy did not just see poverty and hear how it impacted communities. He went out and made sure that we, the American people, knew. He used that information to build the War on Poverty. He used the images, sounds, and stories of the Mississippi Delta to construct a plan, a plan of change. Kennedy raised the social and moral consciousness of the American people. His listening went beyond the stories that the children couldn't even tell him to what politicians could do to change it. He spoke these words to the people so that they could adopt it as a national vision of change:

> And this is one of the great tasks of leadership for us, as individuals and citizens this year. But even if we act to erase material poverty, there is another greater task; it is to confront the poverty of satisfaction—purpose and dignity—that afflicts us all. Too much and for too long, we seemed to have surrendered personal excellence and community values in the mere accumulation of material things. Our gross national product, now, is over $800 billion a year, but that gross national product—if we judge the United States of America by that—that gross national product counts air pollution and cigarette advertising, and ambulances to clear our highways of carnage. It counts special locks for our doors and the jails for the people who break them. It counts the destruc-

tion of the redwood and the loss of our natural wonder in chaotic sprawl. It counts napalm and counts nuclear warheads and armored cars for the police to fight the riots in our cities. It counts Whitman's rifle and Speck's knife. And the television programs which glorify violence in order to sell toys to our children. Yet the gross national product does not allow for the health of our children, the quality of their education, or the joy of their play. It does not include the beauty of our poetry or the strength of our marriages, the intelligence of our public debate or the integrity of our public officials. It measures neither our wit nor our courage, neither our wisdom nor our learning, neither our compassion nor our devotion to our country, it measures everything, in short, except that which makes life worthwhile. And it can tell us everything about America except why we are proud that we are Americans.[9]

Robert F. Kennedy

University of Kansas

March 18, 1968

Robert Kennedy listened with a purpose.

During my days as a community organizer, I went door-to-door to learn about the problems that existed in the communities I served. My goal was to try to become a leader and organize people around the issues that concerned them within their community. One day, I met a woman named Mary who told me she used to work a low-wage job, and the issue that she was most concerned about was health care. She was concerned because she did not have any insurance. After discovering that she was uninsured, I asked, "Why do you think health care is the most important problem in the community?" And she replied, "Health care services cost too much for people to get the treatment they need." As I probed for more information to better understand her situation, she began to tell me the story behind her concerns.

Nearly a year prior to our meeting, Mary had a pain in her stomach, which drove her to seek help in the emergency room. Later, she learned that she had appendicitis. While at the hospital, her appendix was removed before it burst. She knew she had insurance but she never wanted to visit to the doctor for services because of her high $500 deductible. Nevertheless, this time Mary was forced to use her insurance. Her insurance covered most of the health care costs, but she was required to pay the balance for her medical services, a bill of $600. She was a very proud woman who did not want to be in debt to anyone. She prided herself on paying all of her debt, so she purposed to get rid of this medical bill as soon as possible. But because she lived on a limited income, she didn't have enough to pay it. She only had approximately $250 after paying all of her monthly expenses. So, in order for her to pay this medical bill, she knew she was going to have to borrow money.

Realizing her need for a loan, she drove to a local finance business in search of assistance. This business was a short-term lending institution. This company made short-term loans to help people who were in a short-term financial bind. This woman's situation was a clinical definition of a short-term financial fix. This is how the business works: if you give them your free and clear car title, they will give you a loan in cash, but you have to pay the loan back in full within thirty days. If you don't have the full amount due in thirty days, you have to make a monthly interest payment on the money you borrowed. If you fail to pay the loan back, the lender takes ownership and then repossesses your car.

Needing $400 to pay in full her medical debt, she attempted to borrow $400 from this lender. But the business's representative told her they could not help her with a $400 loan because South Carolina law prohibited them from financing $400 at their monthly business rate. They instead offered her a loan for $601. They were allowed to charge their monthly business rate on loan amounts above $600. So she borrowed the $601 from the lender.

Mary was a low-wage worker on a limited income who took at short-term $600 loan at 25 percent interest for thirty days. If in thirty days she did not repay the loan in full, she was required to pay the lender $150 in interest. Mary then explained that because of her illness, she missed time from work, and therefore she didn't have the money to pay her monthly expenses, much less the $601 to pay off this short-term loan. She ended up making ten interest payments of $150. She then lost her job and could not make the eleventh payment; as a result, the business took possession of her car. And as she came to the end of her story, she told me she was now unemployed and without transportation to a job. She believed that if health care was not so expensive, she would not have needed to borrow the money. Then she would have never gotten behind in paying her debts, and she would still own her car.

Even though Mary didn't say anything about working at a job where she didn't earn sufficient wages, it was clear she didn't have income to continue to pay this loan. Also Mary did not say anything to me about the amount of interest she was paying each month, but to me, the interest rate was a serious problem. There was also a problem with the cost of her health care plan—in fact, it could be the reason why she ended up in the emergency room with appendicitis. She had a high deductible and was left with a $600 medical bill.

This situation spoke to me about the need for people to have better access to health care. Listening to her story helped me to better define the problem in the health care marketplace in our state and in our country. This short story became one of the many stories that I encountered many days while working as a community organizer. These stories fueled my passion to promote health care access for those in need. I began to use what I heard to become a better advocate for improved health care in South Carolina and in our nation.

By listening to the stories of the people in the community, I was encouraged to work aggressively to improve the quality of health care for more than a decade. I have worked to find all kinds of solutions to our common problems. I began looking at all kinds of health care issues for the very poor and very fragile. I have studied ways we can provide cheaper, guaranteed, affordable health care for everyone. I did my best to become an expert on these issues for the sake of improving the lives of others. I wanted to be a better leader for people like Mary. I became a vocal advocate and force on health care issues within South Carolina and the nation.

After a decade's worth of work, fighting to improve access to health care, my leadership abilities were recognized on a national level. In January of 2007, I was honored and recognized by Families USA as consumer health advocate of the year. This is an honor that is given to grassroots community leaders who exemplify the highest levels of leadership ability as it relates to being an advocate for consumers in health care. This award is dedicated to the community grassroots leaders who understand the importance and take the time to listen. I was honored and proud to get this award, but ultimately, I knew that the only reason I was able to become a leader on health care was because I learned very early in my career to listen to the people I hoped to serve.

The Voice for Health Care Consumers

FOR IMMEDIATE RELEASE
Thursday, January 25, 2007

Contact: Dave Lemmon
Geraldine Henrich-Koenis
Bob Meissner
(202) 628-3030

ANTON GUNN OF SOUTH CAROLINA IS RECOGNIZED FOR HIS WORK IN SOCIAL JUSTICE AND COMMUNITY ISSUES

Gunn Receives the Families USA Consumer Health Advocate of the Year Award

Washington, D.C. - Families USA, the national organization for health care consumers, presented Anton Gunn with the Consumer

Health Advocate of the Year Award at the annual Families USA Health Action conference.

The award, presented every year since 1998, recognizes outstanding contributions on behalf of our nation's health care consumers. The award was presented to Mr. Gunn for his commitment to social and political issues that affect the people of South Carolina and the country at large.

"Anton Gunn is a passionate advocate devoted to social justice for low-income individuals," said Ron Pollack, Executive Director of Families USA.

Gunn's commitment to social justice began when he graduated from college and started a career as a motivational speaker and social commentator. In addition to his interest in education and social issues that affect young people, Gunn is a community activist for education and health care reform. Gunn hopes that universal health care will become a reality in South Carolina, and he speaks to groups around the state to build community support for this goal. He is also the host of "Front and Center," a radio show where he speaks about social and political issues. In addition, he owns his own motivational speaking company.

Gunn's work carries over into his personal life. He is involved in the faith community. He also serves as a board member of Grassroots Leadership, and he was appointed by the Columbia South Carolina City Council to the Citizen Advisory Committee for Community Development.

Gunn received his bachelor's degree in 1994 from the University of South Carolina and later received his master's degree from the same university. At the University of South Carolina, Gunn founded the University of South Carolina Student-Athlete Advisory Committee, trading in his career as a football player to devote his life to social justice.

--30--

Families USA is the national organization for health care consumers. It is nonprofit and nonpartisan and advocates for high-quality, affordable health care for all Americans.

"Anybody can be great, because anybody can serve."

-Dr. Martin Luther King, Jr

CHAPTER SIX

ESSENTIAL NUMBER 5: MASTER SELFLESSNESS

One essential characteristic that separates transformative leaders from ordinary leaders is their willingness to make the leadership about others, rather than themselves. The ability to selflessly lead an organization, business, or group is an important tool in becoming a transformative leader. Selflessness is a choice. Numerous leaders in the twentieth century lacked the ability or desire to be selfless. Men and women have risen to important leadership positions only to use the position for personal gain and personal enhancement. Their leadership was characterized by selfishness and the grandeur of their own success. Consequently, their twentieth-century leadership style had a negative impact on communities, organizations, employees, and their constituents. This happened because there are stages in the leadership development process when a leader has to choose between personal success and the success of the organization. Many times, ordinary leaders choose themselves over the organization. This breeds distrust and limits the success of the people who follow you. This also reinforces the poor image that leaders have in our society. No one likes to be led by a leader who puts personal advancement ahead of our common good.

In order to be a transformative leader in the twenty-first century, one who would restore the proper image of selfless leadership, you must understand that your leadership is about serving others. It's about using your leadership to put others in a better position. Service should be the first and foremost commitment of any leader who hopes to be a transformative force in the twenty-first century. They must have a strong sense of selflessness and care for the value of humanity. They must be willing to serve with humility.

Leaders need to be committed to making the world a better place. The most transformational leaders who have changed continents, countries, and even cultures have all have been willing to serve the people. Leaders like Mahatma Gandhi and Dr. Martin Luther King, Jr. were transformative because they were willing to serve others. They made sure that the people they reached understood that the mission was not about themselves, but that it was about the people they served. They sought to lead selflessly, and in doing so, they managed to successfully accomplish their mission because they had the support of the people.

In the same vein, anyone who seeks to lead must first understand that service is a prerequisite of leadership. You must be willing to roll up your sleeves and put your hands to the plow. You must be willing to stand side by side with the people you desire to lead so that you can see the world through their eyes—from their perspective. Once you have taken the time to toil alongside them, you will eventually gain their support because they will recognize that you genuinely care about their well-being. Serving those you lead will also cause you to gain a better understanding of how you can improve their lives; then together, you both can work toward securing better lifestyles for all.

WHAT IS SELFLESS LEADERSHIP?

Selfless leadership is critical to world success. If more leaders were willing to serve selflessly, our world would undoubtedly be a better place. Being a selfless leader demonstrates your ability to understand and empathize with people's experiences. As presented in a previous chapter, your personal experiences give you the ability to gain greater vision, and your vision sets the stage for your leadership. Likewise, by serving others you gain valuable experiences of building a bond with those who may one day become the supporters you need to achieve your leadership potential. Also by serving others, you understand the struggles they go through, and you will share in those struggles. It is with this sense of sharing and struggling that you will gain an appreciation of what you are asking others to do when you ask them to follow you in leadership.

Leaders should be willing to serve others long before assuming a leadership position. The process to become a leader begins with service to your community, church, or organization. Service is paramount to successful leadership. You cannot ask people to do something you are not willing to do yourself. In other words, you can't expect your followers to serve you if you are not willing to serve them.

Transformative leaders must also be committed to a purpose higher than themselves. Having the audacity of leadership is about tapping into a higher power. You must recognize that there is something greater happening around you, and this higher power has granted you the gift of leadership. Because leadership is a gift, you must unselfishly share this gift with others. The process of unselfishly using your God-given assets, resources, and strengths to build the strengths of other people epitomizes the purpose of leadership. Your sacrifice and service to others creates an altruistic relationship between you and those you serve. Ultimately, the selfless relationships you develop will demonstrate your ability and willingness to improve the condition of others. As a result, others will be encouraged to follow your leadership.

WHY IS SELFLESS LEADERSHIP NECESSARY?

The word "service" is one of the most used words in any field of human endeavor (e.g., business, community, churches, and politics). Terms like "customer service," "community service," "ministry service," and "public service" are common to most. They have one common denominator—they all suggest that the ability and the willingness to serve is an intricate part of our lives. No person in this world has accomplished anything without the help of other people. We all need assistance from someone at some point in our lives. Therefore, you can conclude that service is necessary for the success of anything that you do as an individual and as a leader. Not only is service critical to leadership, but service is necessary for the general good of society. Whether you're talking about poverty, gang violence, homelessness, world famine, illiteracy, economic disparities, or education, nearly every issue that you can think of is in need of service. There isn't an area on this planet that doesn't require someone to serve—and leadership is no exception. So, transformative leaders should seek out ways to serve.

How Do I Master Selfless Leadership?

In order to tap into how you best can serve the world community, you must be willing to immerse yourself in an issue about which you are passionate or empathetic. We all have a personal issue that touches our hearts or shakes the foundation of our spiritual and moral center. Your goal should be to make a positive impact on this issue even if it's not related to where you are currently serving as a leader. This service activity may take you away from your leadership position, and you may not understand the tangible benefit of this activity. You should understand that this issue needs your help and is worthy of your time regardless of any benefit to you personally. This is called making a sacrifice for others. It is this sacrifice that will have an impact on the issue. You have to realize that everyone needs help sometimes, and a transformative leader is always willing to understand that his or her role is to help people all the time.

In your act of service, you will have to uncover what you have to offer. What resources are at your disposal? Do you have an hour, a week, or a month to volunteer? Do you have money you can contribute? Do you have professional skills that could be useful? We all have some talent, time, or treasure that we can contribute to improving our world. I challenge you to find a way to share your gift in a personal, hands-on way.

When you have discovered the issue you want to positively impact, and the gifts you are going to use to make that impact, you need to take action. As you volunteer your services, take note of those around you. Who shows up to help you? Who else is committed to help on this issue? What people need your help the most? You should build relationships with them as you work together to provide meaningful service. As we will learn, strong relationships are necessary to become a transformative leader. Building these strong relationships with other caring individuals is important. Working hard at serving people who need help on that issue or in that community is also important. You should make a personal long-term commitment to help. Long term means for an extended period of time like several months, a year, or several years. Your service can't be transactional; it should be a deep commitment, a commitment that you are willing to make without any gratitude or recognition for the talents, treasure, or time you have given. You are not serving to be recognized and applauded for your effort to the group or issue. You are serving because leaders should serve.

Real leadership is about understanding power. Our world is a power-hungry place. Some only seek power for the sole purpose of obtaining it. Others seek power only to abuse it. But what if power was gained for the sole purpose of helping other people? By serving other people, you have the power to change someone's world. So when you use your power for good, it helps build power in other people. I learned the rules about power during my time as a community organizer working at South Carolina Fair Share. In our grassroots organizing training session, called Lovely Acres,[10] we teach communities the Three Rules of Power:

Rule #1: Power rules.

Rule #2: Power flows through people.

Rule #3: Leaders build power in others.

Helping others to build power to help advance their own causes is an important step for your leadership development.

Here is where the rubber meets the road. In order to be a transformative leader, you must be willing to share your power with others. It is imperative that you use your power for the betterment of others. When you do this, you and the people you serve are guaranteed overall success. Serving does not have to mean ladling out soup in a homeless shelter; it can, and does for many. But service can take the shape of whatever form you envision. Look out your office window. Is there a need there that you can meet? Fill it! Does a story on the evening news shock you? Change the situation! There is a need for selfless service all over our world. There just aren't enough people who are willing to provide the service. Mastering Selflessness is a mission!

Consider answering the following questions at this time:

What causes or issues are you passionate about? What stirs you to action? What do you have to contribute to this passion? Time? Resources? Talent? When will you begin to contribute your services?

STORY OF THE TRANSFORMATIVE LEADER

No matter what your religious beliefs, the historical character of Jesus stands out as the ideal example of a person who dedicated his time on earth to selfless leadership. The adult ministry of Jesus was devoted to the service of others. Hungry people were fed. Poor people were served. People cast away from society were included. Spiritually empty people were filled. And what did Jesus gain from this service? He gained a group of devoted followers who set themselves to continuing his mission for more than 2,000 years after his death. Isn't that what every leader desires? We want people to continue the work that we start, even when we are no longer here to lead them. Selfless leadership is the way to create that kind of following.

Jesus is said to be the dividing point in history. Not only is time divided into before and after Christ, but people are also categorized by their beliefs regarding him. Why is that? I think it is because his work still inspires people. Service gives birth to true wisdom. Wisdom leaves an impression that will not fade, a legacy in the lives of people who have been changed for the better and tell the story. The story gets told and retold, creating inspiration. Selflessness not only changes individuals, it changes whole cultures. Now, that is leadership. That is selfless leadership!

Many people know of my work in politics, social issues, and even youth development, but very few know of my work with homeless men. It has always pained me to see adult men walking the cold and lonely streets in the cities of our country. Some of them are on the streets because of some tragic event in their lives. Others are homeless because of mental illness, addiction, or a criminal past. There are even others who are homeless by choice. Regardless of the reason, I believe that everyone should have a place that he or she can call home. It is painful for me to see people without a home.

We all have walked along the street and seen the homeless in our community. We have walked by them. We have stepped over them. We may have even given them change from our cars and our pockets in an effort to be a Good Samaritan. But have you ever wondered what happened in that person's life that led them to being homeless on the street? I have wondered often. I also wanted to encourage these individuals to get help and maybe even a path to get off the streets. So for the last twelve years, I have spent time working with homeless men. I don't volunteer at shelters, churches, or soup kitchens, although these are noble and important resources for the homeless. I choose to work with them on the streets.

When I am in any city or any town and I am approached by a homeless person and asked for change or money for food, I take the opportunity to have a personal conversation with the individual to help figure out how I best can help them. I want to know why that person needs spare change for food. I ask questions about how he or she ended up on the streets, the last place the person remembers living, and lastly, other than money, what I can do to help him or her get off the streets? Most people I encounter on the streets are shocked that someone wants to hear their story before giving them spare change. Others are even more shocked that I am seriously trying to help them find a better way to live. Regardless of their response, I try to use my knowledge of community resources and other community leaders to help get them off the street.

Over the twelve years I have been doing this, I have learned a lot about how life can take you in a bad direction that is hard to recover from. I have met military veterans, Katrina survivors, and even a former schoolteacher. This is why I count my personal blessings every day. If it were not for God's grace in my life, I could be homeless too. I have also learned that not every homeless person wants my help, nor do they want to be engaged in a twenty-minute one-on-one conversation. There are some, however, who are very grateful for just taking the time to listen. Others are grateful for my financial assistance, but most of them are overwhelmed that I provide both an ear and a means to deal with their immediate needs. I have even helped some to leave the streets, even if it was only temporary. Nonetheless, I believe that if nothing else, I provided some small level of assistance to people who are living in some very difficult circumstances. I believe that I have had an impact in the lives of the hundreds of individuals that I have met over the years. I don't have a good measurement of the significance of the impact at this point, but I strongly believe that someone, somewhere, is better for the service I have provided. I know at the moment that I was helping them, many of these men said to me the two most important words in the English language: "Thank you." That is the entire acknowledgment that I will ever need to know I had an impact.

"I am the greatest; I said that even before I knew I was."

-Muhammad Ali

CHAPTER SEVEN

ESSENTIAL NUMBER 6: HAVE AN EMCEE'S ATTITUDE

As a twenty-first-century leader, you must have the willingness and the ability to share your message with those who may oppose you or your vision. There are times when, as a leader, people will not immediately embrace where you envision them to go. There are also other times when people will vocally disagree and even offer a vision different from what you proclaim for your group, organization, or community. As a leader, you must always respect those who oppose your vision in leadership. You should not only respect them, but also be willing to continue to offer your vision to them. There are times that as a leader, those who oppose you may become the key to your success. As a transformative leader, in the face of knowing the opposition, you must be willing to share your vision with those who do not understand or support you. This essentially means you have to be willing to preach to the nonbelievers in your world. As you work to make progress in your given area, there will be skeptics, doubters, and people in general who will oppose what you are trying to accomplish. You must accept the fact that not everyone will share your vision. But you must not let people stop your willingness to share your message.

As a transformative leader, you must understand that some people will not automatically embrace you as a leader. There may be others who will not accept the vision you have provided as a leader. Your leadership may also be criticized and even rejected by those who disagree with your vision. Having the attitude of a transformative leader means that, even in the face of rejection and criticism, you have to be willing to go into the lion's den to present your vision (and sometimes defend your vision) to the opposing team. You must be willing to walk into possibly hostile environments to share your vision with those who may not respect your leadership. To overcome this adversity, you must develop a resilient mentality. You must be prepared to verbally and intellectually engage in a battle of ideas with those who oppose you. You must be prepared to share with others your point of view and your philosophy as a leader. You must also be willing to face the criticism of those who don't agree with your philosophy. To successfully win this battle of ideas, you must infuse yourself with greatness. This greatness is an attitude that cannot be given to you by other people, you must have it within yourself. You have to believe that you are the greatest—the greatest leader, the greatest visionary, and the greatest in whatever you do, and wherever you go. You must be willing to develop the attitude of a hip hop emcee.

THE EMCEE'S ATTITUDE

When hip hop music began in the late 1970s and early 1980s, all rappers (sometimes known as emcees, or master of ceremonies) thought they were the greatest rappers in the entire world. They had a vision about hip hop, and they believed themselves to be the kings of that vision. All rappers believed that they had the skills and the ability to be the king of the hip hop world. Emcees had the mentality that they were the greatest entertainers in their lifetime. They were bold. They were self-assured. They had audacity. They believed what they had to say would make them the leader of the hip hop culture through the next millennium. All emcees wanted to be the leader, and they expected others to follow the example that they set. Each individual rapper had this mentality about his or her musical abilities. Each one thought he or she had the best rhyming skills in the world and that if others just had the opportunity to hear him or her, they all would agree.

Oftentimes, emcees would test their greatness by using their rhyming skills to challenge other great rappers to lyrical contests called battles. A battle would be a public contest similar to a duel or a debate to allow onlookers to judge who was the better rapper. The two opposing rappers would battle each other in open venues. Again the goal of the battle was to prove who had the skill to potentially earn the title of best emcee. Rappers would look at these battles as activities to prove their greatness and challenge others who thought they were great. The victor in these rap battles was always determined by the audience that was present to see the contest. Oftentimes, these battles took place in the home community of one of the emcees. In effect, certain emcees had a "home field advantage," if you will. In their home community, a crowd would be biased against the visiting emcee. Their bias played out in a way that would strongly support the emcee with whom they were more familiar. Many times in the rap world, the difference between being a great emcee or a good emcee was your willingness to prove yourself in places that were not friendly to you. Greatness meant you had gumption to travel into someone else's home turf and work hard to prove your rapping supremacy over that person in front of his or her fans. Once you proved to the crowd that you were the better emcee, you would immediately gain the respect and support of those fans, thus exponentially increasing your fan base.

This happened because of the unwritten rules of battling—Rule Number 1: After a battle, you have respect for your opponent regardless of who won the battle. Rule Number 2: If you are the winner, the respect you gain could at a minimum add new fans to your support base, and at a maximum, you could get your opponent to join you. In essence, you could potentially get the defeated rapper to collaborate with you. Both of you together could accomplish more than either of you could individually.

Like emcees, new leaders should always be prepared to share their vision of their leadership with those who may not support them. This allows you to prepare yourself for the dissenting arguments against your vision. It also allows you to speak to people different from you, so that you can better understand their concerns. Sharing your vision with your opponent is very important as you seek to build a team of leaders who will ultimately help you achieve your goal as a successful leader. As we will learn in Chapter 9, having other leaders to challenge your leadership will help you master the audacity of leadership.

In addition to boldly displaying your leadership skills, like emcees, twenty-first-century leaders should be willing to go into hostile territories, to win the hearts and minds of people with opposing views. A good emcee knew he could only claim true rapping supremacy if he went into hostile territory and gained the respect and admiration of the people there. Emcees would not be afraid to leave Brooklyn, the Bronx, or any of the boroughs of New York City to go to Atlanta, Miami, Los Angeles, Dallas, or Oakland to try to gain respect from the hip hop fans there. And to gain their respect, these emcees had to have flawless rapping skills (vision, commitment, authenticity, listening skills). They had to connect with their audience. So before making their presentations, they would gain an understanding of the issues that were culturally important to the group of people they were performing for. Leaders should understand this lesson; it is always important for a leader to know what is culturally relevant or important to the group that you are speaking to. They had to understand the perspective, lifestyles, and concerns of the foreign crowds in order to win them. People do not care what you know, until they know that you care. And in leadership, if people know that you care about their position, they are more likely to listen to what you are offering them as an alternative.

THE IMPORTANCE OF AN EMCEE'S ATTITUDE

As a leader striving to embody the audacity of leadership, you must go into hostile territory to share your vision. You have to show that you are willing to learn and understand the perspective of others, particularly those who oppose you. Your goal is to gain the respect of your opposition. You don't ever want to ignore people, especially people who may not share your perspective. Instead, you should always acknowledge your opposition and respect their position. If you take the time to acknowledge their voice, they will be more apt to give you an opportunity to verbalize why your vision is better suited for the task at hand. It is your opportunity to create a change in their position. It is like the process used in political debate; with respect and decorum, each side is given ample opportunity to present its vision for leadership. Once both parties are given the opportunity to share their vision, those looking for leadership can decide which vision is better for them. In this process, ideally, you could have some naysayers find the merits of your vision and your leadership. The people who initially may be naysayers and opponents could become supporters of your vision because you presented your arguments to them. These would be supporters that you would have never had if you had not spoken to them. By speaking to them, you could gain some very important converts, who at times can be among the most faithful people in your camp. They are faithful because they have tested your leadership by being skeptical. This is just like an emcee on the battlefield, being tested by the audience for his or her lyrical skills, so being an audacious leader, you would also be put to the test by opponents. They may not initially support all your ideas, but by sharing your vision and leadership, you can change their hearts and minds. Sharing your ideas with those who oppose you is one of the most powerful examples of having the audacity of leadership.

Sometimes, you won't be able to win them over. But at the very least, you will have earned their respect for your willingness to communicate your vision in the face of opposition.

STORY OF A TRANSFORMATIVE LEADER

President Barack Obama campaigned that he was an effective leader to bridge the differences between varied demographic groups. He also campaigned that he had the vision and the integrity to bring people of opposing views together to solve problems in our country. As he campaigned on this vision of unity, he hoped to show everyone that he was the kind of leader, greater than any other, that could unite those with the most differences between them.

Since his election, President Obama has strived to embody the role of a uniting leader. One incident in particular is a perfect example of what having an emcee attitude can do for you. In 2009, the president received an invitation to be the University of Notre Dame's[11] commencement speaker at graduation in 2009. He was asked to be a commencement speaker and to be honored with an honorary doctorate degree from Notre Dame. The thought of being the speaker is not of any great shock, because every university would want the president of the United States to be its commencement speaker. But this invitation by Notre Dame was a particularly odd invitation for President Obama to receive because of his philosophical differences with the teaching at the university on the issue of abortion. The president believes in giving a woman the right to choose whether to have an abortion. The university, a fundamentalist Catholic institution in the United States of America, believes that abortion is wrong and supports the position of outlawing abortion in America.

The president and the university had totally opposing views on this issue. There were many who did not welcome President Obama because of his position. There were even more who did not support him being given a degree at the graduation of an institution where people upheld all of the values as Catholics in United States of America.

The president had the opportunity to ignore this invitation and ignore those who are different from him. Or he could accept the invitation to speak to people who are different to try to find a bridge on which these two opposing views could work together to share their voice on this issue. He accepted the invitation to speak at the University of Notre Dame. Facing intense protest from 2,500 students, scrutiny from all media sources, and opposition from political pundits who do not share his position, the president had the audacity to accept the degree and be the commencement speaker. In his speech, President Obama maximized this opportunity by laying out a vision of how the role of public discourse and valuing people who are different from you is the most important factor to consider on the topic of abortion.

After his speech, the president was met with applause and support from members on both sides of the issue. They were all rightly offended, but they also were all rightly supportive of what he had to say. He took that opportunity to try to bring people together by creating an open space, where both sides could dialogue about this issue. And while he is a leader who has the ability bring people together to discuss the issues that separate us, he also has the ability to find ties that bind us together.[12]

The president was bold, focused, and committed. He believed that he was the best possible leader to give this speech. He had the leadership skills necessary to convey a message, but his objective was not to convert people to his side of the issue. In the end, he managed to gain the respect of those who disagree with him because he was willing to face his opposition. To become a transformative leader, not closing the door on an opportunity to dialogue on an issue is just as important as, if not more important than, supporting your own position on that particular issue.

In 2008, I ran for the South Carolina House of Representatives—this was my second attempt at this position. The district I hoped to represent covered two different counties. Some neighborhoods proved to be supportive, while others were not very welcoming of my candidacy. Overall, I found that it was not that they were against me as a person; instead, they did not share my political philosophy or positions on some issues. They opposed the fact that I ran for office as a Democrat; they traditionally supported Republican candidates. Some were not fond of my firm belief in supporting public schools. Others had difficulty accepting my push for increased funding for infrastructure in South Carolina.

While campaigning, a voter invited me to meet with her neighbors who were interested in the two candidates running for office (my opponent and me). This neighborhood had not been particularly kind to Democratic candidates in years past, but regardless, I was always very happy to visit voters, no matter where they lived. So I took her up on her offer to meet with her neighbors in an effort to learn what was important to these neighbors, and share my political philosophy. My goal was to let them know why I was the best candidate running for office that year. I immediately assumed that because we lived in the same district, we were all the same, we cared about the same issues and agreed on the solutions to these issues. But upon examining the voting records of the community, I learned that I had very little in common with this community. The people there voted differently than I did. Nonetheless, I went to her house meeting, expecting that I would not have a lot of support. The host of the house meeting had previously informed me that all of her neighbors were Republicans, including her husband. They did not vote for Democrats; in fact, they never voted for Democrats, because they did not share the political ideology of Democrats. So my opportunity to visit with them was a chance for me to speak to people who some would consider my opposition. I was extremely excited about meeting with this Republican group because I had the confidence and belief that I was the better candidate for the job. I felt that no matter who you are or what you looked like, regardless of the color of your skin, and your background, if you gave me the opportunity to speak, I could earn your support. In essence, I embodied the attitude of an emcee. My goal was to present my arguments as effectively as I could, but I was prepared that I might not gain any new supporters in my quest to become state representative.

So as expected, after being introduced, I was asked to state why I was running for office, at which point I clearly voiced my reasons for pursuing my positions. I told them what I hoped to accomplish, as well as my concerns. I unashamedly explained that I was a public school supporter. I told them I believed that we needed to raise the cigarette tax for the sake of improving health care. My overall message was that I was in support of good government. Good government means that it should be responsible to the people that government should work for the people and that all people should participate in the government as voters and critics; this ensures that government is made up of the people.

I did my best to learn what was important to this group by talking to the host and researching the voting patterns of the community. I was solidly aware that they had a somewhat different philosophy. However, I did not know that the majority of the people there either sent their children to private schools or home-schooled, so naturally they were not supporters of public schools. And some of them were also cigarette smokers who did not want the price of cigarettes to be increased, because it would be raising taxes on a specific group of people. So needless to say, I gave my strong, progressive, political message to a group of people who were totally opposed to my views. However, despite their initial opposition, because I took the time to communicate, not only did they come to respect me, but by the end of that evening, I managed to gain some voters who had never voted for a Democrat before.

Many people may question why I thought it necessary to speak with voters who did not share my ideology. To them I would say it is beneficial to embrace your opposition along with your supporters. You have to be willing to go into the skeptics' camp to state your claim. You must be willing to share your vision against all odds. In doing so, you will create an opportunity to convert some naysayers into believers.

"Leaders have to give time for relationships. But more demands will be placed on their time as they become more successful. So if a person's success is based on developing relationships, then they have to continually find new ways of getting it done."

-Coach K (Mike Krzyzewski)

CHAPTER EIGHT

ESSENTIAL NUMBER 7: LEAD THROUGH CONNECTION

A great leader must understand that quality leadership is about relationships—it's about building connections with people. These connections must be meaningful. Oftentimes, we hear the phrase, "There are six degrees of separation between most people"; that is the idea that, if a person is one step away from each person he or she knows and two steps away from each person who is known by one of the people he or she knows, then everyone is at most six steps away from knowing any other person on earth. These six degrees of distance keep us from knowing and having a relationship with every person on earth. This idea shows you that there could be a minimum of six barriers between you and the person you do not know sitting beside you at the local coffee shop.

A wonderful organizational consultant and friend, Moss Blackmon, coined the phrase "six degrees of connection" to negate these six degrees of separation. It was Moss's belief that the members of all organizations should strive to find connections with those they work with to achieve their common goals. In accordance with Moss's advice, as a transformative leader in the twenty-first century, you must turn the six barriers of separation into bridges of connections. For some people, keeping this distance is a healthy dose of privacy. It is privacy that keeps everyone from knowing the intimate details in your life. But for you to have the audacity of leadership, you must learn how to take the example of six degrees of separation and create six degrees of connection. These six degrees of connection are not as simple as building a relationship with everyone on earth, but building at least six dimensions of your relationship with those you work with in your leadership position. As a bold new leader you should seek to find six things you have in common with every person you meet. Your goal as a leader is to find out what you have in common with other people. Then you should use those commonalities as a foundation to build a better working relationship. Six commonalities can be the minimum amount of common ground between you and the individuals you intend to build a relationship with, but don't allow yourself to be limited—the more you have in common, the better your working relationship.

Once you have developed genuine relationships through common bonds, you will find that the people you are connected to will be some of your strongest supporters during the good and bad times. Instead of viewing you as a leader removed and disconnected from their life experiences, they will view you as a friend connected to them—one who shares in their joys and empathizes with their pains. Ultimately, you will both share an allegiance to each other. This is important because people do not quit on the ones they care about.

The audacity of leadership is about developing strong individual relationships with individual people. It is about creating seemingly unbreakable bonds with the people you work with. It is the understanding that having genuine relationships is paramount to quality leadership. People follow, support, and lift up those they know well. So in order for others to follow your lead, they must know you well. The six degrees strategy can be used as your intentional plan to get to know people.

SIX DEGREES OF CONNECTION

Six degrees of connection, simply put, is building individual relationships. The essence of this is trying to find six points of connection with the person you intend to form a relationship with. A relationship built on six points of commonalities will not be easily forgotten or broken.

If you were interested in dating someone who worked at a doughnut shop, but you hated doughnuts, would you still go into the shop? More than likely, you would because you would seek out every opportunity to spend time with that person. If you had to eat an occasional doughnut or just order a cup of coffee every day, you would do it because your actions would be a means to an end. You would do whatever it took to secure your chances of getting to know the object of your affection. In the same vein, transformative leaders should have the same amount of enthusiasm for building relationships with the people they have teamed with to ultimately change the world.

Spend time doing what they enjoy. Get to know them and find what you have in common with them. All relationships will not be deep, but by finding common ground with people, you let them know that they are important to you. A connected leader will encourage people to develop the tenacity to run the extra mile because they will realize that they are building a genuine relationship, not just for the goals you are trying to accomplish, but also for the meaningful lifelong relationships they will obtain.

BUILDING BONDS OF SIX DEGREES

As you are spending time with your team, or spending time serving various communities, you should be looking for opportunities to build individual relationships beyond the scope of work you are involved in. Your goal should be to develop genuine bonds with new individuals and associates. In order to accomplish this, you must have one-on-one conversations with them. In fact, in the profession of community organizing, it is extremely difficult to get people organized toward any change unless you have a relationship with them. Great leaders know they must be intentional about creating opportunities to develop relations with people.

One way to develop relationships is to conduct twenty-minute relational meetings with each individual who wants to join your team. Your goal is to build an initial connection and determine what will motivate that person to stay involved. Your goal is to hear his or her story. Listen to what inspires or compels him or her. Whether it's done over coffee, lunch, or dinner, leaders must work to build relationships with people based upon their self-interests. I believe that quality time is more important than quantity time. Do not just focus on a twenty-minute meeting; focus on identifying each individual's personal strengths and weaknesses as they relate to your leadership vision. Look for aspects of each individual's life that is similar to your life. Do you share the same birth date? Are you both movie buffs? Do you both have the same educational expertise? Do you share the same faith? Look for commonalities that would help build a foundation of relationships with them.

After completing the initial meeting, you should conduct a longer, more visionary follow-up meeting to assess each individual's willingness and interest in helping to achieve your vision. At the same time, you should be focused on learning more about that person in order to build deeper connections. Essentially, your main objective of your leadership development is to identify six different ways you and the person you intend to form a relationship with are connected. There should be a minimum of six ways you are connected.

Then you should conduct a third meeting to focus on your joint strengths because it will play a role in activating your vision. By considering each other's strengths, you will then be able to better determine how that individual can participate in bring your vision to life. The audacity of leadership gives average people a blueprint to contribute their talents to our society as transformative leaders. The goal of this leadership model is to help new leaders achieve extraordinary things for the world community. As an effective leader, you should always offer others an invitation to become a transformative leader. Their acceptance will be the basis of getting them to do something that shows their commitment. The connection within the six degree strategy is based upon the demonstration of one's actions toward the goals.

As the old Asian proverb states, "The journey of a thousand miles begins by taking the first step." Using the relational meetings to identify a person's self-interest, a leader must get others to plan and take the first step with them. This is a step that must be comfortable to the person, but it must also be a small step toward your desired vision. As a leader, you must assist each individual with developing his or her personal "work plan" within the plan to achieve the desired outcome.

Ultimately, your objective is to find new team members that can fill in the gaps within the plan that are not being filled by other individuals in your organization. Together, we establish the timeline and time frame for completing the plan. Each individual then carries out his or her own work plan within the larger work plan.

THE IMPORTANCE OF SIX DEGREES STRATEGY

It is fairly apparent that this kind of attention takes a lot of time. And you will find yourself asking, Is it worth it? What does this kind of relationship building accomplish? But the essence of success is based on personal relationships between people. In short, your legacy is built by people who know you. Leaders who take the time to develop meaningful relations with others lay the foundation for a strong community. A group of three is certainly stronger than one individual. But a group of three individuals moving in three different directions has no strength! A community united first by a singular purpose is strong. A community held together by a clear purpose and relationships is indestructible.

By developing the personal within the larger group, you can shape your blueprint for carrying out methods to achieve your desired outcome. The kind of leader who will change the world will be connected and never alone. Followers will respond with more togetherness. Bring them into your circle to work on a problem, and the relationship will last beyond the solution.

STORY OF A CONNECTED, TRANSFORMATIVE MILITARY LEADER, GENERAL COLIN POWELL

In his autobiography, Powell tells a story about how he took pains to be accessible to the troops during his Army command. Every afternoon, he walked the same route at the same time, deliberately setting himself up to be ambushed (his word). It wasn't long before people with problems realized that this was a golden opportunity to get the boss's ear— and they took full advantage of that opportunity.

At the same time, Powell adds, he made it clear to his immediate subordinates that he had no intention of using his little strolls to undermine the chain of command. This was, he emphasized, simply a good way for people to blow off steam, and perhaps even convey a great idea in an unfiltered form. The noncommissioned and junior officers got the point and stopped worrying about open lines from the bottom of the pyramid to the top. "If anything," Powell recalls, "my outdoor office hours gave them a chance to blow off steam, too."[13]

During the 2008 presidential primary campaign, it was my job to find out why people liked or supported Senator Obama. Every answer was different. Some liked his diverse background. Some liked his religious affiliation. Some liked that he was a Democrat. Others liked his stand on a particular issue. I then probed deeper to get to their main reasons so that I could connect with each individual. If Senator Obama would never meet those people face to face, they would need to have a personal connection with someone involved in the campaign. I became that person.

I met Phillips through my work campaigning for Senator Obama. We didn't know each other in the least when we met, but after just a few conversations, we found six points of common experience:

1. Barack Obama. We both were involved in his presidential campaign at the beginning.
2. New kind of politics. We were both believers in putting people above political parties.
3. Lost a brother. We both knew the pain and the healing.
4. Writers. He completed a book and I was working on my book.
5. We were both greater than six foot, three inches tall.
6. We both had run for public office.

Phillips and I may not ever become best friends, but we have maintained our relationship beyond Barack Obama's campaign. In fact, it was only my hope that on Election Day, Phillips would remember his connection to me and that I played a role in that election process. In fact, Phillips has remembered me far beyond that election. Phillips always pops into my life when it comes to other political endeavors he has pursued. Whether it was business, political, or community work, Phillips and I have an important relationship that I believe will never be broken.

Six Degrees with Malik

In 2005, Malik and I met, seemingly as total strangers. It appeared we had nothing in common. We had no intention of becoming acquaintances, much less friends. Our connection was strictly business focused. He was responsible for planning an event for the college where he was employed. He needed a professional speaker for one of his college's leadership programs, and I fit the bill because I'm a professional speaker who focuses on leadership. Malik asked me to speak at his event. This was quid quo pro. Nothing more than meeting each other's business needs—a favor for a favor.

But as an audacious leader, I was immediately interested in his management endeavors of a college-based leadership development program. I immediately thought, "Could Malik help me to advance my desire to help train and develop the next generation of community leaders? How could he become a part of my vision to develop more positive leaders?"

After spending twenty minutes with Malik, I learned so many degrees of connection that helped us build a relationship on a deeper level. Here are just a few aspects we discovered:

1. A decade earlier, we attended the same undergraduate university, at the same time no less.
2. We both took classes in the same major and in the same building, but didn't know each other.
3. We both shared several friends, but were never introduced to each other.
4. We both are the oldest of four children
5. We both are married and the father of one daughter.
6. We both are lovers of hip hop music and culture.

These six degrees were just the beginning to a connection and commitment toward leadership development. In general, we both have a shared vision around progress, politics, and people, and we were going to join forces.

Following our newfound connection, we worked toward building a team that supports our shared vision of changing the world through new leadership. The relationship with Malik and our team is what gave birth to the principles that later became these essentials of twenty-first-century leaders. Malik has helped me filter my thoughts on leadership because we built a relationship to understand each other and the beliefs that we shared. We have a shared sense of purpose and commitment. This is what unites us even though we share different personalities, knowledge, skills, and abilities. Malik and I are still working to change the world, one leader at a time. This is what six degrees has done for me. And I firmly believe that the six degree strategy will enable you to identify and strengthen the relationships that will help you change the world.

"Never doubt that a small group of thoughtful, committed people can change the world. Indeed, it is the only thing that ever has."

-Margaret Mead

CHAPTER NINE

ESSENTIAL NUMBER 8: BUILD A LEADERSHIP TEAM

In order to achieve your leadership greatness, you need to surround yourself with great people. As a matter of fact, your success as a leader hinges on the level and quality of the leadership team you have around you. As an audacious leader, you must surround yourself with other audacious leaders. The audacity of leadership is about building a community of leaders from which you will draw support, motivation, validation, and clarification. Essentially, these people will make up your leadership team.

If you want to ensure your success, you must seriously take into account the need to build a significant leadership team. I am not talking about a team of people who follow you to help you work toward success; rather, I am referring to a leadership team filled with other leaders. You must build a community of other leaders who are working to accomplish their goals in other professional fields. This team should not be a group of "yes men" and "yes women."

They should be people who will challenge you and push you to your leadership limits. This should be a team of people who can gain new knowledge from each other; so as each leader grows wiser, the leadership team grows wiser.

Building a leadership team is about grounding your leadership in others. As discussed in Chapter 3, people will quit on a job, they will quit on an idea, they will quit on a program, and they will quit on a project, but they will not quit on people. You have to build a community that won't quit on you so that you will not quit on them. This community is your leadership team.

CREATING A LEADERSHIP TEAM

As is said in sports, the difference between a good team and a great team depends on the individual people making up the team. Nothing is more important than making sure that the *right* people are on your team. The right team of leaders consists of leaders who bring balance to your leadership experience, as you bring balance to their experience. This balance in leadership will create strength. For example, if you are the leader of a large corporation with thousands of employees, you may have a vision, commitment, and all the other qualities necessary to practice audacious leadership, but who can help keep your leadership strong? A leader in this position should rely on other leaders to help keep him or her strong. So having a pastor of a large church organization on your team could be critical to keeping your corporate leadership strong. This pastor may have as many members at her church as you have employees at your major corporation, or the pastor can help strengthen your faith and spirituality, so you stay grounded in your leadership. Likewise, an athletic coach who has the skills and experience in motivating their players to give their best at all times, can strengthen you in motivating your managers or your employees at the corporation. Collaborating with these leaders is invaluable. You can strategize together, plan together, debrief together, and ultimately grow together. As your team moves forward toward improvement, so will you. In fact, this concept is support by the Bible scripture,

Proverbs 27:17, which reads, "As iron sharpeneth iron; so shall a man sharpeneth the countenance of his friend."

More importantly, your leadership team should establish a culture in which all members honor a commitment to support each other. You should meet with your entire team on a regular basis and have one-on-one meetings with your key leaders to help you prioritize your objectives so that you can stay focused on your goals, while establishing stronger working relationships. Together, you will build a task list of goals and objectives, and develop activities for your leadership team to accomplish. The team that works together, stays together. As the leader, you must remain focused on the mission of materializing your vision, because in doing so, you will improve the depth of your ability to lead your team.

You should also know it is okay to openly share your perspective, goals, fears, worries, and concerns with other members of the team. In so doing, you will create bonds of trust and define the path you intend to pursue. While you are in the preliminary stages of a mission, your leadership team can help you with ideas of how to accomplish your goals, overcome your fears, and address your worries and concerns. You are more likely to accomplish your endeavors by joining forces with your team to refine the game plan for your organization, church, group, or business.

Members of a leadership team are not clones. In fact, the more versatile they are, the more vibrant the community will be. These differences may make working together very challenging at times, but the uniqueness that each one contributes is worth the effort. However, members must work in unity as it relates to helping accomplish the mission. Welcoming diverse individuals who are unified for the sake of accomplishing one cause is a recipe for success.

When you begin evaluating other people's strengths and weaknesses, you need to be very aware of your own. If you and another team member have the same strengths, one of you will have to tone it down to give the other room to work. Your strengths can become weaknesses to the team if members are too much alike. So in addition to seeking out other leaders, you must also strive to find people who complement each other.

Also be wary of assumptions you make about others. Don't assume that people know how to help you. You must examine your own strengths and weaknesses as well. Do not let others make assumptions! Assumptions mean details are open for misinterpretations. Misinterpretations can be detrimental to building a leadership team. To avoid misinterpretations, always ask clarifying questions so you can understand how your team believes they can help you.

THE IMPORTANCE OF BUILDING A TEAM

It may seem more time efficient to master leadership on your own. Expediency may trump synergy in your mind. But let's take a moment to consider that assumption. Christians believe that Jesus was God incarnate. The power of God walking around in the flesh could have surely handled what needed to be done all on his own. I'm sure his expediency would have wowed us. But instead of being a loner, he chose twelve ordinary guys to work with him. Not twelve super-educated, well-spoken men, but twelve grassroots, blue collar workers. He entrusted them with the secrets of humanity and divinity. Why? I can think of several reasons. Jesus remained focused on the mission by constantly having to communicate and redefine it for the twelve disciples. When you have to continually create new ways to share your mission with people who may not understand your stance, your ideas tend to become more transparent to you.

True success is measured in the people who get deeply involved and get invested to help you accomplish the mission. It is one of the basic rules of community organizing. The more people you get involved and invested to solve a community problem, the more attention it creates on the community problem, which makes more people want to solve the problem. The more people you have trying to accomplish the same mission, the more power you have to keep the mission going!

As Doris Kearns Goodwin notes in her book on Abraham Lincoln's political rivals, an effective leadership team has "real participation in which individuals acquire a sense of belonging, a sense of dignity, a sense of self-confidence, and a realization which grown-up people must achieve if they are going to step even halfway out of their childhood, and that is that nobody is going to take care of their problems except themselves. It means an organization which is a welding of those interests in a community crucible heated by a fanning of interests, enthusiasm, dreams, passion, ambitions, and determinations into a citizen's pressure bloc—into an articulate representative organization whose strength is recognized by all civic authorities for what it is, and therefore they will respond to this pressure."[14]

I cannot think of a better way to share what it means to have a leadership team than this quote. The team, at its core, must be focused on responding to the pressure of getting better. It is the pressure of getting better as a group that will help you to get better as a transformative leader.

When Abraham Lincoln was elected president of the United States, he was virtually unknown. Having served only one term as an elected official, Lincoln was also relatively inexperienced in governing. When it became clear that he had won the election, his hometown of Springfield, Illinois, celebrated far into the night, but Lincoln did not join the party. Instead, he sat in his private study, overwhelmed with the weight of a country on the brink of war on his shoulders.

> "I began at once to feel that I needed support," he noted later; "others to share with me the burden." As the exhausted townsfolk shuffled back to their homes and the city "sank into its usual quietness," Lincoln began to compose his official family—the core of his administration. "This was on Wednesday morning," he revealed, "and before the sun went down, I had made up my Cabinet. It was almost the same as I finally selected."
>
> On a blank card he wrote the names of the seven men he wanted. At the center of his list stood his chief rivals for the nomination—William Seward, Salmon Chase, Edward Bates. The list also included Montgomery Blair, Gideon Welles, and

Norman Judd, a former Whig. While several months would pass before the cabinet was assembled, subjecting Lincoln to intense pressure from all sides, he resolved that day to surround himself with the strongest men from every faction of the new Republican Party—former Whigs, Free-Soilers, and antislavery Democrats.[15]

Lincoln knew the value of surrounding himself with those who were more politically experienced than he was. These men represented varying political ideologies. But they united around one central theme—they all wanted to save the Union. Each had influence over a different sect of Congress. Each held sway with a different geographical area of the North. Each wielded his power, within his sphere of influence, to accomplish their goal. It was Lincoln's decision to build this team that played a strong role in keeping our nation together through the Civil War. And ultimately, this team played a significant role in making Lincoln one of the strongest presidents in the history of the United States of America.

Every audacious leader needs a base of like-minded, goal-focused individuals to accomplish specific objectives. Identifying a community of interest from which you will draw support, motivation, validation, and clarification is the beginning of your leadership team.

Having a good leadership team grounds you to stay focused on accomplishing the goals and objectives of your organization. The team will also keep you focused on your mission. Your members will challenge you to stay true to your internal motivations and increase the impact of the desired change. Your leadership team measures the significance of your mission. The better the people on your leadership team, the greater impact your mission will have on your organization.

My Leadership Team

As a professional, I have tried to make the most of my leadership. There is one thing I have learned over time: I am only as good as the people I surround myself with. I was fortunate to learn this lesson early in my life. Since that time, I have always focused on connecting myself with those who are doing better than I am doing.

Whether it was playing football and basketball in the yard with older, more athletic and experienced players or learning how to be a great community organizer from veterans of the civil rights movement, I was always close behind and learning from those leaders' experiences. As it relates to sports, I would say my success as an athlete can be attributed to the other great players that I surrounded myself with. I was always the younger player working out with, hanging out with, and learning from the upperclassmen. I emulated their workout habits, their playing styles and techniques, and their mannerisms. I figured if they were starters in every game, the worst I could do is serve as their backup. However, if I applied the lessons I learned from them to my own talents, I could become the starter. I took what I learned from them and ultimately perpetuated their legacies within my own success.

As it relates to my career as an organizer, I am truly standing on the shoulders of those organizers who came before me. I spent as much time as possible reading, studying, and learning about some of the greatest community organizers in history. Whether it was Jesus Christ, Martin Luther King, Jr., Saul Alinsky, Si Kahn, Ella Baker, Fannie Lou Hamer, or Paul Wellstone, I wanted to learn as much as I could about their work. Many of these organizers had mastered the art of training and instilling leadership in other people. It is from these other organizers that I learned to improve myself. I did everything in my power to get involved in organizing training programs, internships, fellowships, and workshops. I was blessed to get into several programs. I was even more blessed to come out of these experiences with amazing mentors who would serve as a part of my leadership team. Consequently, my leadership team is comprised of several experts who often serve as a sounding board to challenge all of my thoughts, ideas, successes, and failures. This team is extremely important to me because they provide critical feedback for my intended steps. The feedback they offer is virtually invaluable because it comes from their ability to channel their own personal successes, failures, and ideas to help me to center my leadership style. And because they already walked the roads that I aspired to trot, just having their advice almost always guaranteed my success.

This leadership team has become a special group in my life. They help me with business decisions, political decisions, and personal decisions. I learn a lot from these people, and they often keep me from making mistakes. When I do make a mistake, these are the people who help me get back on my feet. These leaders are the people who influenced me to consider running for office, and this same team also encouraged me to become the youngest executive director to lead a statewide nonprofit organization in South Carolina. And as I write, I am reminded that it was my team members who helped propel me to write this book.

But what's more noteworthy about this team is that each member has achieved his or her own individual mission through individual leadership teams. My leadership team includes a three-time published author, a recording artist with nine best-selling albums, a college professor, a ground-breaking entrepreneur, a top federal government official, a veteran political campaign operative, and a parent of outstanding children. This team is well accomplished and very diverse. Each person on my leadership team has excelled in an area of life that I hope to improve in. Each one of them has provided me an example of success that I hope to emulate in order to achieve similar or greater success. All of these people have taught me something along the way that has motivated me to tenaciously pursue success. I am so grateful for my team, and I believe you can build a leadership team that will help shape, develop, and strengthen your endeavors as you practice audacious leadership.

"If your actions inspire others to dream more, learn more, do more, and become more, you are a leader."

-John Quincy Adams

CHAPTER TEN

ESSENTIAL NUMBER 9: DEVELOP THE NEXT "YOU"

A transformative leader, who dares to lead audaciously, recognizes that successful leadership is not solely dependent on your vision, commitment to authenticity, or willingness to build a team. Your leadership efforts are cemented by what you leave behind. Others should be able to measure the strength and impact of your leadership long after you are gone. So to ensure longevity, you must take the time to nurture the next generation of leaders while you lead. Some say imitation is the most sincere form of flattery—so, there's no greater flattery than demonstrating your success through the imitation of your leadership abilities by those who will continue your legacy.

Great leaders must understand that their leadership is directly connected to the future—what they are doing now will benefit immediate and future recipients. If you examine some historical leaders, it is clear that those who have experienced success in leadership were the ones who were willing to leave behind a framework, blueprint, and philosophy for other aspiring leaders to follow. These leaders also invested their time to help other aspiring leaders learn and grow. They shared with these aspiring leaders opportunities and information that would advance their development. By investing in these aspiring leaders, a transformative leader will build the skills of others to surpass the existing leadership abilities of their leader. By setting a precise example while they are acting as transformative leaders, others will be able to effectively and successfully assume their leader's role long after their leader has moved on. It's like the owner of a business teaching his or her child how to run the business while the child grows up, and when the parent has retired, the child has the knowledge of the business's model but also has the youth and vitality to take the business to a higher level.

In the same vein, twenty-first-century leaders should share their wisdom with aspiring leaders. In doing so, they will help develop future leaders so that they could, in turn, perpetuate a positively changed world. But if a leader fails to pass on his or her leadership practices, the living legacy he or she built in the organization will inevitability be erased in death. This death is not just expressed in a literal death; it can be a figurative death. If a person does not grow his or her leadership, he or she is only killing the possibility of his or her leadership in the future.

IMPORTANCE OF DEVELOPING THE NEXT GENERATION

As this fast-paced world continues to change, the lifespan of leaders continues to shrink. While leaders work harder and longer to accomplish their missions, their dedication often leads to quicker burnout. Thereafter, that leader is no longer effective, because his or her progress is stunted. So in preparation of this eventual burnout and total exhaustion, it is important that as a leader, you find other promising leaders to share your burdens, philosophy, and more importantly your experiences. Transformative leaders begin to prepare other leaders for leadership in anticipation of their own eventual demise. I can't think of anything that is more important than developing leadership skills in people who don't have them (as defined by this book). We will always need more great leaders in this world, and it is the responsibility of our current great leaders to help prepare them for leadership in the future. There is an old phrase that says, "Dig your well long before you are thirsty." This phrase is a good descriptor of what transformative leaders should be doing to prepare their organizations for their future leadership needs.

You must actively prepare future leaders by sharing the key principles for transformative leadership. They must first understand what they must become—a leader with a vision. They must also understand that they are developing a strong power base for themselves by being an apprentice in a leadership setting. Creating this power base will take the young leader to so many new places and new heights, but he or she must be prepared for these experiences, just as you were prepared for your experiences. A leader prepares for new leadership experiences by allowing others to share in his or her experience. This sharing of leadership experiences creates a positive cycle of leaders actively investing in new leaders. This investment perpetuates a positive cycle of transformative leadership. It is this vision of a perpetual transformative leadership process that truly builds new confidence of the public in our leadership institutions.

As we learned in Chapter 6, the rules of power are very important to become a transformative leader. You must be selfless in your leadership. A great way to demonstrate your selflessness is to practice the rules of power in developing the next generation of leaders. It is particularly important for you to master the third rule of power. You must take the time to develop the leadership skills of others. If you fail to pass down the wisdom you learned as a leader, you probably should not be a leader in the first place. If you do not work to develop leadership in others, you deprive future generations of the potential benefits of what you have accomplished. So it is imperative that you strive to mentor aspiring leaders so that they can continue to change minds, ideas, and the world through the missions in operation.

Your mentees will become some of your most loyal followers because they will count it as their personal responsibility to continue what you have started. These people will listen to your every word and partake in the change you create. They may not have the skills, experience, or intelligence to go where you have gone, but it is your responsibility to see past their shortcomings. It is your responsibility to help them to become better leaders. You must create an environment where people get excited about becoming better leaders. Your job is to find a team of young people, four or five individuals, that you can surround yourself with so that they can bear witness to your leadership practices. You have to give them a chance to see what it is like to be you. Keeping your mentees close will also give you an opportunity to support their leadership development. Transformative leaders must be model leaders. Many people practice what they see. In fact, most of us learn about 90 percent of what we know from what we see. So if you want your mentees to develop the qualities of a leader who is selfless (who gives back), you need to demonstrate that trait. If you want people to be dedicated, then you must show them your commitment. If you want them to put these principles first, you need to put them first.

A LEADER WHO BUILT THE NEXT GENERATION

You may not be privy to the intricate details and masterminds behind professional football, but most everyone is familiar with the name Bill Walsh. Walsh was a legendary college and professional coach, who was known for creating a play-calling system on the offensive side of football which led to multiple victories for his teams. Coach Walsh is recognized as a transformative leader in the world of football. He won three Super Bowls; he took college teams to championships; and he changed how the game of football was played on offense and defense. The new offensive system that he created is known as the West Coast offense. It is one of the most difficult offenses to learn as a player, but more importantly, it is even more difficult for opposing teams to stop. This system, under his leadership and direction, was the reason his teams won three Super Bowls and ultimately changed the game of football forever.

The second and most important thing that Bill Walsh is known for is the legacy he created through his leadership. Walsh was not only a great coach for developing football players, but he was also a great coach for developing other coaches. More than twenty current or former NFL head coaches can trace their leadership in coaching to the lineage of Bill Walsh[16]. Bill Walsh recruited young, inspiring, and motivating coaches who were willing to learn about his system within strict disciplinary parameters. He then taught his system with great emphasis, and his assistants grew to mirror his discipline. By sharing the technique behind his leadership success, Walsh became a picture-perfect example of the benefits one can experience by sharing one's success with promising leaders. The men who have coached under Walsh and learned from his overall leadership have gone on to become some of the greatest and most famous coaches in NFL history. Among them are Dennis Green, Sam Wyche, Mike Holmgren, George Seifert, Ray Rhoads, Brian Billick, David Shula, John Fox, Mike Shanahan, Steve Mariucci, Sean Payton, Joe Bugle, Pete Carroll, Jeff Fisher, and Tony Dungy. Each one of these coaches has reached the pinnacle of his coaching career by either coaching in or winning a Super Bowl or college national championship.

Bill Walsh revolutionized the lives of these young leaders. He taught them everything he knew, and like Walsh, these coaches are also sharing what they have learned from him with others. So while Walsh is gone from this earthly setting, the legacy he created and shared will continually live on.

I have invested, and always will invest, in the next generation of leaders. I wish that I could say I learned this from my mentors and role models; but I did not. I believe that I have always understood the importance of what it means to invest in young leaders. I guess you could say growing up the oldest of four boys was where it all started. Living with three brothers, we were always competing against each other in sports and games. I never wanted to lose to my brothers, and they strived to always win against me (rarely did they have success). I prided myself on beating them in every competition. However, I could not stand the thought of any of my brothers losing to someone outside of our family. I wanted my brothers to be the best they could be against all other competition. I encouraged them to be the best and taught them everything that I knew in sports and games. I also taught them everything I knew in real life. I never wanted them to make the same mistakes I made. So I took it upon myself to train them and compel them to be their very best.

I still carry this mentality with me in everything I do. This is why I constantly take advantage of the opportunities I am given to speak with students in elementary schools, middle schools, high schools, and colleges. I consider it my duty to inspire young people to want to follow in my footsteps. I see it as a major responsibility to train and compel young people to be transformative leaders. In one year on average, I speak with twenty-five different groups of students. In all of these meetings, I tell a very authentic and personal story about how I have become the person I am. After I share my story, several students often ask if they can be a part of my world. When asked, I make it my responsibility to try to make their request a reality.

For the last ten years, I have strived to enlist one to three interns in my office. Each time, I give them the opportunity to really live in my shoes. I include them on my conference calls, my meetings, and my scheduled events, and two of them have even helped to write this book. It is my hope that they will use the information they gained from my mentorship to eventually accomplish and exceed the things I have done in my lifetime, long before they reach my age. It is my hope that they will continue my legacy while developing a legacy of their own.

I believe that I've been commissioned to make our world a better place. So not only do I position myself to be the change I desire to see in the world, but I also encourage my mentees to do the same. Together, we will make a world of difference. I believe that I am building this legacy by becoming, first, a model for what I want to see in the world.

"We have also come to this hallowed spot to remind America of the fierce urgency of Now. This is no time to engage in the luxury of cooling off or to take the tranquilizing drug of gradualism."

-Dr. Martin Luther King, Jr.

CHAPTER ELEVEN

ESSENTIAL NUMBER 10: TAKE EXPLOSIVE ACTION

As you embark on your journey to audacious leadership, it is my hope that you will find guidance in the essential skills addressed herein. Hopefully, this book will provide a blueprint that will seal your fate as a transformative leader of the twenty-first century. But your fate as a transformative leader is contingent upon your willingness to embrace the last essential, take explosive action. For what good is a leadership blueprint if you fail to implement the plan? Taking explosive action is the final important step an aspiring leader must employ to transform the twenty-first century. Taking this kind of action will bring you closer to making a difference.

Some believe there are three types of people in the world: People who wonder what happened, people who know what happened, and people who make things happen. Transformative leaders make things happen by taking explosive action. But in order to make things happen, you must learn *when* to take action. The ability to act timely on the opportunities presented to you is what separates transformative leaders from mediocre leaders. You should understand that if you have confidence in your vision, demonstrate your commitment and honesty, listen to the people, serve others, and build relationships with your followers and other leaders, you will secure the foundation you need to accomplish your long-term goals. At this phase, all that is left to do is take action. You must immediately move forward with confidence, knowing that you have the skills necessary to succeed. Transformative leaders must recognize the urgency for timely action, and then they must act.

All successful leaders take explosive action because they instantly apply what they learn. When they learn something, they act on it. They also learn from their mistakes. Successful leaders figure out what works and what does not work, then they actively apply what they learn. Most of us do not apply what we learn, and as a result, we repeatedly find ourselves at the same disappointing positions. What separates great leaders from average leaders is that great leaders, in any given field, learn how to use the information they are given to achieve greater success. There is not a huge gap of time that goes by from when a transformative leader learns new information and when he or she applies that information. Most people in leadership are often afraid to apply what new information they have learned. They are afraid to try it because they are afraid of failure. But what these leaders should recognize, more than anything else, is that knowledge without application is useless. You must be willing to take action regardless of failure or success. If you talk to successful leaders in any field, particularly in business, they will tell you that a significant part of success lies in just getting the job done. Many times, a challenge or goal may seem unattainable, and the pressure of completing the tasks at hand may become so overwhelming that it may cause you to quit on the project. But transformative leaders maintain their composure and take explosive action to accomplish the task. The goal is to function and thrive under the pressure, no matter what the situation.

A leader learns to thrive under pressure by getting comfortable with being uncomfortable. It is constant discomfort in taking action that builds a leader's stamina to endure difficult situations and excel in leadership. Therefore, you must be willing to put yourself in difficult circumstances to really grow into becoming a transformational leader. If you do not step up to the plate, you will cost yourself the opportunity to excel as a transformative leader.

Taking explosive action also requires you to stay focused. You must rid yourself of all distractions. In order to remain centered, you must focus on your immediate goal. Avoid getting caught up in the accolades of leadership when you take action. There will always be people who want to celebrate the fact that you have taken a leadership role. It is easy to accept constant congratulations and well wishes of others and get caught up in your immediate success. If you achieve any success and get distracted by your success, you run the risk of only achieving that goal. There is a phrase in coaching sports, "You are only as good as your last victory." If your last contest was a win, you may hope to stay right there to be celebrated and remembered by others as a winner. This win should not be the focus of the big picture when taking explosive action. Instead, you should purposefully carry out the long-term plan. Stay focused on your Daily Method of Operation. Expand your vision, and recruit people to your team who will help you achieve the big picture. You must take it one step at a time. To ensure the success of your leadership, it's critical that you learn how to focus on the specific task at hand, but always take action toward the next step.

Next, you must have the ability to recover when your actions create a problem. Great leaders will make mistakes, but the difference between a great leader and an average leader is that a great leader learns to recover quickly from his or her mistakes. Mistakes will always occur, but you have to be willing to address them quickly, learn from them, and move on. Do not dwell on your past mistakes. Instead, figure out how you could use the mistake as a teachable moment to learn what you can do better, so you have a successful outcome the next time.

The one thing that is difficult to avoid when you are trying to be a bold, transformative leader is the daily grind of trying to make change. Sometimes, the road to change gets so hard that you begin to make excuses for not taking action. As a transformative leader, you must work hard to avoid making excuses for why you cannot do something. Avoid making excuses for your lack of resources. A transformative leader will always find another way to get what he or she needs to be successful. Working in politics, I have learned that things do not always go your way, and it's easy to find an excuse why they didn't. You can either choose to accept the excuse or you can improvise, adapt, and overcome the obstacle. As the old adage says, "There is more than one way to skin a cat." You can accomplish and overcome those barriers that some may think are unattainable; it's just going to require your resourcefulness. If you have too much on your plate, then get a bigger plate. If you don't have enough money, then get a second job. Think about all the stories of successful people who had to manage full-time jobs and demanding families while planning, working, and hustling in their own business on the side and at night. You must be driven just as they were driven. It may not always be easy, but you can always make a realistic plan to accomplish your goals by utilizing the Daily Method of Operation, which we learned about in Chapter 2.

Some people may wonder, don't you need courage to take action? You don't need courage. Courage is only the willingness to confront and manage your fears. Everyone, even the most successful person at any level of leadership, is afraid at times. You haven't experienced life if you have never been afraid of something. This fear is something that all of us feel at one point or another. The main difference between transformative leaders and those who are not is the fact that transformative leaders confront their fears and accomplish the goal anyway.

Finally, forget about the *haters* in your world. A hater is a naysayer or a detractor to your goals and dreams. Haters can manifest themselves in your coworkers, your friends, and even your family members. They may have experienced a failed dream of their own, and because misery likes company, they may directly or indirectly try to deter you from pursuing your goals. But do not entertain them, rather use their skepticism as the force to drive you forward; make it a part of your vision and commitment process. Your goals and dreams are yours. You should always work for them and fight for them. Do not ever let other people stop you from taking action and steal your dreams and goals by sharing their cynical and negative attitudes. In time, your dreams will become your reality, and the haters who thought you could never do it will be left wondering how you did it. And once you've established yourself as a transformative leader, this is the point to move on; this is the point where you can set more dreams to get greater results.

In all organizations, there are those who take some action, and a few who take explosive action. In my experience with leadership and personal goals, those who take explosive action will be leaps and bounds ahead of the rest. They are the ones who are most able to handle change. It is as if they know that explosive action will get them to the destination faster, and more effectively, while simultaneously empowering others along the way to be the change they desire to see. These people know that the doubters and haters cannot hinder their success. So they deflect their negativity and use the energy to motivate their cause.

Above all, stick to your dreams and *take explosive action* on them, because without them, our world would wallow in mediocrity. The world needs you to be a transformative leader. You must take explosive action to become what the world needs.

CHAPTER TWELVE

Conclusion

So if you are still asking, what is the ultimate purpose of this book? The purpose of this book is for you to first ask yourself the question, do I want to make a difference in the world? If the answer to your question is yes, then the ultimate purpose of this book is to give you my perspective on what it takes to make a difference in this world as a leader. It is also to show you that if you apply the ideas that I have shared in this book, you can become a leader who not only makes a difference, but you can also become a leader who transforms the world we live in.

If you have answered yes to the question, you are most likely already a good leader. You don't have to become governor, president, CEO, or senior pastor, or be given a title, to be a leader. All you need to do is decide to take responsibility for a part of your community—this is what real leaders do.

In our current society, we need more people who are willing to make a difference. Many times, most people think they don't have what it takes to become a great leader, and their present leaders are doing a good enough job. Well, neither of these assumptions are true. There is plenty of room in this world for more leaders. The idea that one super leader will take care of all the problems in our community is a MYTH. Malcolm, Martin, JFK, and Gandhi are all gone. More importantly, one leader can't possibly solve all the complex problems that our communities face every day. So the more transformative leaders we have, the more problems we will solve. We need YOU to apply these principles, gain a broader perspective, and get the *audacity* to work on the problems within our churches, businesses, communities, and halls of government.

Each of these areas will require a unit of transformational leaders to handle them. We need women, young people, poor people, and people with disabilities, and many others to become transformative leaders instead of just followers. We need the audacity of leadership from all walks of life in order for our society to truly live up to the ideas that we richly and rightly profess.

So my message is, please don't wait to lead. It's just possible that you are the one who will make the move toward creating the change that we are looking for. Transformational leadership is a role that was made for you. Remember, you are the one, and the only one, who can decide what kind of leader you would like to be in your corner of the world. Go ahead and dare to take hold of your dreams to do the work that is meaningful to you. You have the ability to make significant changes in the lives of the people with whom you work, live, and play. The power is in your hands and in the pages of this book.

But if you have come this far and have not found anything that I have shared in this book to be useful, then we have wasted our time together. Wasting time is what no true leader can afford to do. I hope you will pass this book on to someone else that you think could get some meaning and use from these pages.

Either way, I thank you for your commitment to leadership, learning, and sharing the essentials that have made such a difference in my leadership experiences.

I leave you with a lyrical verse from one of the greatest hip hop emcees of all time, Rakim, from the title song of his album, *Follow the Leader:*[17]

>**...Then after that I'll live forever—you disagree?**
>**You say never? Then follow me!**
>**From century to century you'll remember me**
>**In history—not a mystery or a memory**

These are some of the deepest thoughts in hip hop lyrics about leadership. These are thoughts that enter my mind every day that I live in the audacity of leadership. The message of what a generational impact you can make if you embrace *The Audacity of Leadership*. I think there is a message in these lyrics for all of us who hope to make a revolutionary difference in this world.

Looking forward to seeing you on the road of transformation. Good-bye and God bless.

ACKNOWLEDGMENTS

This book would not have been possible without the inspiration from my family and friends. I want to begin by thanking Lenora Bush Reese. Lenora is a wonderful mentor who deserves tremendous recognition. I am grateful to her for being my first example of a transformative leader, and for giving me my first opportunity to become a transformative leader. Lenora gave me my first job as a community organizer. She began mentoring me on the first day at work and, for the last decade, has remained a wonderful and strong influence in my life. I have learned so much from her great character, and I have been very privileged to work directly with such an amazing woman.

I would also like to especially thank Juanell Teague, a wonderful woman of God who truly is a servant leader. I am glad to call her my friend. She spent months in 2006 guiding me to clarity about my vision for this book. Her team of professionals helped me find my voice by taking me through a process that allowed me to tap into my experiences that became this book. I appreciate all of her hard work, dedication, and time committed to helping me become a better professional.

I want to also express my great appreciation to Chuck D, Eric Carlson, David Coryell, Myron Terry, Jerry Inman, Dr. John Ruoff, Charlene Sinclair, Jennifer Henderson, Deepak Bhargava, Si Kahn, Dr. Arlene Andrews, Dr. Owen Connelly, Ronnie Johnson, Nancy Johnson, Jeff Weber, Stacey Brayboy, Steve Hildebrand, Steve Corboy, Trav Robertson, and Barack Obama. All of these individuals have played a significant part in helping me develop the audacity of my leadership. Without all of your experiences in my life, the manifestations in these pages would not be possible.

I would also like to thank Nelecia Murrell, Eddie Oakley, Angela Douglas, Sam Johnson, Heyward Harvin, and Malik Whitaker, all of whom read and provided feedback in regard to the book. These individuals took the time out of their busy schedules to provide me with editorial advice.

Last but not least, I would like to thank my parents, Mona and Louge Gunn, and my brothers Jamal and Jason, for giving me the upbringing and family that has helped to define who I am as a person. It is because of you that I have had the ability to develop into who I am. Thank you.

APPENDIX

Audacity Exercise:
Vision: If I had unlimited resources, unlimited support, and unlimited time, how would I change the world:

_____

_____

_____

_____

_____

_____

_____

_____

_____

_____

_____

_____

_____

_____

Commitment: What are the ten things I need to do to be a better leader in my field of operation?

1._____

2._____

3._____

4._____

5._____

6._____

7._____

8._____

9._____

10._____

Authenticity: What are the five things about me that will never change and that will help others to understand who I really am?

1._____

2._____

3._____

4._____

5._____

Listening: What are five things I will do to become a better listener?

1._____

_____

2._____

_____

3._____

_____

4._____

_____

5._____

_____

Becoming a Selfless Leader:

What causes or issues am I passionate about? What stirs me to action? _____

_____

_____

What do I have to contribute to this passion? Time? Resources? Talent? _____

_____

_____

When will I begin to contribute them? _____

_____

Emcee's Attitude: I believe that I can become the greatest leader in my field (profession/organization).

These are the five things I will accomplish to prove that I am the greatest leader:

1._____

_____

2._____&_____

3._____&_____

4._____&_____

5._____&_____

My Leadership Team: Who are they? Why?

These are the seven people I would like to model some aspect of my life after and the thing I admire most about them:

1._____&_____

2._____&_____

3_____&_____

4._____&_____

5._____&_____

6._____&_____

7._____

Daily Method of Operation (DMO): Daily questions to ask myself.

Where do I see myself in five years as a leader? _____

_____

_____

What are the things I need to accomplish each year to reach my five-year goal? _____

_____

_____

_____

_____

_____

What am I going to do today to get closer to my annual goal that will ultimately get me to my five-year goal?

_____

_____

_____

_____

_____

_____

_____

_____

_____

The Next Generation:

Who are the five young people I would like to see become great leaders?

1._____

_____

2._____

_____

3._____

_____

4._____

_____

5._____

_____

What things will I do to show my support, and how can I invest my time in long-/short-term mentorship?

_____
_____
_____
_____
_____
_____
_____
_____
_____
_____
_____
_____

For more information on Anton J. Gunn and his motivational programs, products and services, contact:

www.AntonGunn.com

or

Send correspondence to
Top Gunn Associates, LLC
Attn: Anton J. Gunn
P.O. Box 290820
Columbia, SC 29229
803-667-3944

ABOUT THE AUTHOR

Anton J. Gunn is a well-respected speaker who has been featured in print, on television, on the radio, and in front of live audiences both domestically and internationally.

He is recognized as one of the top under-forty community leaders in America. His career spans more than a decade of doing grassroots, community-driven political leadership development work. From beginning his career as a college football player turned community organizer, Anton has reached the highest levels of leadership in politics and organizational management. Anton has used his skills and experience to become one of the strongest voices for progressive change in America.

Anton has worked with leadership executives in education, health care, economic development, and the telecommunications industries. He has assisted businesses, local government and state leaders, and even President Barack Obama.

Anton has been featured in *The Los Angeles Times, The Wall Street Journal*, and *The State Newspaper,* and *Time* magazine hailed him as "a Leader in Obama's Grassroots Army." He also has appeared on ABC's "Good Morning America," CNN's "The Situation

Room with Wolf Blitzer," "Your World with Neil Cavuto," and "CBS Evening News." In 2009, Anton was the focus of an international news documentary produced by the Japan Broadcasting Corporation (also known as NHK).

Anton is also a public servant. In 2008, Anton was elected to serve in the South Carolina House of Representatives. Anton is the first African American leader in history to represent his district.

Prior to his election, Anton was the state political director for Barack Obama's 2008 presidential campaign in South Carolina. Anton's role was to provide political leadership and guidance to then-Senator Obama during the South Carolina Democratic primary election. As a result of Anton's work, Obama was successful, winning 55 percent of the vote in the primary election.

Anton's thirteen years of professional experience has garnered him recognition as one of the top under-forty community leaders in America in 2006. His list of honors and achievements include 2008 Community Change Champion Award, Center for Community Change; Consumer Health Advocate of the Year, Families USA, 2007; Southern Rural Development Initiative, 2006 Top Ten in the South Honoree; Alumni of the Year, University of South Carolina College of Social Work, 2006; 2001 Faculty Award, University of South Carolina College of Social Work; 2001 Student of the Year, 2000 Emerging Leader, National Congress for Community Economic Development.

Anton J. Gunn is the president of Top Gunn Associates, LLC, a South Carolina-based consulting firm. Top Gunn Associates works hand-in-hand with clients to develop and implement winning strategies for leadership development, management, politics, advocacy, organization empowerment, and education.

Anton holds a B.A. in History (1994) and a Master of Social Work (2001) from the University of South Carolina, where he lettered in Division I college football. Anton is a member of the National Speakers Association, the National Association of Social Workers, and Kappa Alpha Psi Fraternity, Inc. He resides in Columbia, South Carolina, with his family.

In addition to being an author and leadership consultant, Anton delivers his message *The Audacity of Leadership*™ through keynotes, seminars, workshops, and retreats across the United States.

FOOTNOTES

(Endnotes)

1   Wellstone, Paul. www.wellstone.org.

2   Public Enemy. "Contract on the World Love Jam." *Fear of a Black Planet*. Def Jam Records, 1990.

3   "Theodore Roosevelt 26." About the White House: Presidents. www.whitehouse.gov/about/presidents/theodor-eroosevelt/ 1 April. 2009.

4   Obama, Barack. *The Audacity of Hope*. Crown Publishers, New York. 2006._

5   Connelly, Owen. *Blundering to Glory: Napoleon's Military Campaigns*. Rowman & Littlefield, Maryland. 2006.

6   Obama, Barack. *Dreams from My Father*. Crown Publishers, New York. 1995,

7   The Bible: Proverbs 1:8.

8   Remarks of Senator Barack Obama at the Robert F. Kennedy Human Rights Award Ceremony, Wednesday, November 16, 2005.

9   Remarks of Robert F. Kennedy at the University of Kansas, March 18, 1968

10 South Carolina Fair Share. Lovely Acres. 1990: comm-org. wisc.edu/syllabi/lovely.htm

11 *Los Angeles Times*. Editorial: "Notre Dame's Obama Flap." April 1, 2009: www.latimes.com/news/opinion/editorials/la-ed-notredame1-2009apr01,0,4893557.story

12 Baker, Peter and Saulny, Susan. "At Notre Dame, Obama Calls for Civil Tone in Abortion Debate." *New York Times*. May 17, 2009. www.nytimes.com/2009/05/18/us/politics/18obama.html

13 Harari, Oren. *The Leadership Secrets of Colin Powell*. McGraw-Hill, New York. 2002, p. 35.

14

15 Goodwin, Doris Kearns. *Team of Rivals: The Political Genius of Abraham Lincoln*. Simon and Schuster, New York. 2005, p. 280.

16 Gay, Nancy. "Bill Walsh Planted the Ultimate Coaching Tree." *San Francisco Chronicle*. July 30, 2007.

17 Rakim, and Eric B. "Follow the Leader." *Follow the Leader*. MCA Records, 1988.

Lightning Source UK Ltd.
Milton Keynes UK
UKHW040036220422
401880UK00008B/285/J